CHAPTER

The FINAL CHAPTER

S. MAXWELL CODER

Tyndale House
Publishers, Inc.
Wheaton, Illinois

Unless otherwise noted, all Scripture quotations are taken
from the King James (Authorized) Version.

First printing, November 1984
Library of Congress Catalog Card Number 84-51319
ISBN 0-8423-0866-0, paper
Copyright © 1984 by S. Maxwell Coder
All rights reserved
Printed in the United States of America

To my beloved wife
BETTY
the most remarkable woman
I have ever known, whose unfailing love,
constant encouragement, and help
have made possible my Christian service
and the writing of this book.

CONTENTS

PART THREE:
THE FUTURE OF THE CHURCH

PART FOUR:
FINAL DESTINY

PREFACE

This is an account of the astonishing biblical record of what the future holds for the human race. Much has been written which tries to show how current events are predicted in Scripture. But many writers have strayed from the biblical record, resorting to speculation and imaginative fiction. It is not easy to find a complete, conservative treatment of what the Bible actually says about the end times.

The prophetic record is complex, touching every aspect of what lies ahead. *The Final Chapter* discusses twenty-six themes in prophecy in an attempt to provide a comprehensive picture of what is predicted for the world and its inhabitants—the living and the dead.

This book is based on material I have presented at Bible conferences at scores of churches in recent years. It was written because of the great enthusiasm shown by congregations which had not previously heard Bible prophecy based on the actual words of the prophets.

Any work of this kind is likely to be criticized because some passages of Scripture appear in more than one chapter. However, this is unavoidable if every theme is to be given a complete treatment. For example, verses dealing mainly with the second coming of Christ are also needed for an adequate discussion of subjects such as the great tribulation or the kingdom of Christ.

I have presented Scripture quotations in such a way as to let them speak for themselves, and to comment on them as though they mean what they say. If I sometimes fail to accurately summarize the teaching of the prophets, it is because no student of the Word of God, regardless of how careful and deliberate, can find the "perfect" language with which to phrase the limitless content of the Bible.

This book is based upon the premillennial, pretribulation-rapture view of Scripture, held by professors at Moody Bible Institute and at most of the world's Bible schools. Portions of the material dealing with Israel—the land and the coming kingdom of Christ—are largely condensed from my earlier book, *Israel's Destiny* (Moody Press, 1978). I have added an appendix to aid the increasing number of lay persons who want to examine the Scriptures for themselves.

S. Maxwell Coder

The Jews . . .
the Gentiles . . .
the church of God.

1 Corinthians 10:32

PART I
THE FUTURE
OF ISRAEL

CHAPTER 1
THE PEOPLE OF ISRAEL

The Bible divides the human race into three parts: the Jews, the Gentiles, and the church of God (1 Cor. 10:32). The Jews are the people who descended from Abraham, Isaac, and Jacob. The Gentiles include all people who are not Jews. The church of God is made up of all Jews and Gentiles who have trusted in Jesus Christ as personal Savior.

It is remarkable that the Jewish people should be mentioned in this threefold division of mankind. They form only a small part of humanity, they are scattered everywhere over the face of the earth, and they are often disliked and persecuted. The mystery of the Jews' prominence deepens when we discover that four-fifths of the Bible—the only book written by God—is devoted to them. The history of the human race for the first two thousand years is condensed into the first eleven chapters of Genesis, but the history of the Jews is given more than one thousand chapters. Many think the church is of supreme importance, but only the last fifth of the Bible is given to its origin, nature, doctrines, and destiny.

One does not have to read very far in the Bible to learn why the Jewish people are given so much attention. When all of mankind rebelled against its Creator and fell into sin, God called one man, Abram, to help him begin a divine program for bringing humanity back to righteousness. God promised Abram that his descendants would bring blessing to all the families of the earth (Gen. 12:3). Abram became

Abraham, father of the faithful. Abraham was made progenitor of the Hebrews, through whom God gave to the world his Word and the Savior of mankind, and who are destined one day to rule the world under the Messiah.

At the call of God, Abram left his home in Ur and traveled to Canaan, where he had a son, Isaac. Isaac's son Jacob, or Israel, had twelve sons, the founders of the twelve tribes of Israel. When these tribes were still small (a total of about seventy people), they were taken to Egypt to become slaves. There they multiplied greatly, then returned to their land four hundred years later. By the year 1000 B.C. the people of Israel had become a powerful and victorious nation under King David. Persistent sin later brought divine judgment. The kingdom split into two parts.

The northern kingdom, called Israel, was conquered and taken captive by Assyria in 721 B.C. The southern kingdom of Judah was defeated and led away captive to Babylon in 586 B.C. In the days of Ezra and Nehemiah, forty-two thousand Jews returned to their land. Their descendants were in Palestine when Christ was born. Following the destruction of Jerusalem by the Romans in A.D. 70, the people of Israel were dispersed all over the world, where most of them remain today.

Israel became the only nation on earth to have its history written in advance—a remarkable outline of its future was given to Moses (Deut. 28–30). This God-given record is developed and expanded in other Scripture passages. Because Israel is the only nation to have descended from one man, its people are regarded as the purest-blooded, proudest-descended race on earth. They are remarkable for their antiquity. Authentic documents trace them back to more than two thousand years before Christ. The Roman Empire is regarded as ancient, but when the prophet Daniel was writing about its future, the city of Rome was nothing but a village of huts on the banks of the Tiber. Israel then had been a nation for 450 years, and a distinct people for one thousand years before that.

These people, hated by enemies who have sought their destruction ever since they first appeared, have been miraculously preserved. Their continuing existence can be explained only by the place God has given them in the divine program. They have seen empires rise and decay. No nation has ever prospered in their land, but they have prospered in all lands. The world does not realize it, but the Jews are the key to human history. This astonishing statement is found in Deuteronomy 32:8: "When the Most High divided to the nations their inheritance, when he separated the sons of Adam, he set the bounds of the people according to the number of the children of Israel." No student of world events can afford to be ignorant of what the Bible has to say about the Jewish people.

Long ago God gave to the Jews the "power to get wealth" (Deut. 8:18). Their wisdom is proverbial. Joseph became prime minister of the land of Egypt. Daniel was given a place close to the king of Babylon. Solomon was the wisest man who ever lived. Jews have occupied places of leadership in every field. Today they are prominent in science, medicine, art, literature, music, business, and industry.

For nearly two thousand years after the Jewish people were scattered among the nations, "the wandering Jew" found no safe haven, no place of rest and security. Two sentences from the prophetic Word summarize their long and bitter experience: "Thou shalt become an astonishment, a proverb, and a byword, among all nations whither the Lord shall lead thee. . . . And among these nations shalt thou find no ease, neither shall the sole of thy foot have rest: but the Lord shall give thee there a trembling heart, and failing of eyes, and sorrow of mind: and thy life shall hang in doubt before thee; and thou shalt fear day and night, and shalt have none assurance of thy life: in the morning thou shalt say, Would God it were even! and at even thou shalt say, Would God it were morning! for the fear of thine heart wherewith thou shalt fear, and for the sight of thine eyes which thou shalt see" (Deut. 28:37, 65-67).

Near the middle of the nineteenth century the Jews of Europe began to feel that the time was drawing near for their return to the land God promised them. Theodore Herzl called the first Zionist congress in 1897 in an effort "to create for the Jewish people a home in Palestine, secured by public law."

A few years before, the study of Bible prophecy had become popular. Soon the lost doctrine of the second coming of Christ was rediscovered. Conferences on Bible prophecy began to be held. Bible institutes were founded. A number of famous Jews turned to Christianity. The great Jewish Bible expositors appeared on the scene, and the modern Jewish missions movement began. Increasing numbers of Jews returned to the land.

In 1925 Israel's flag flew for the first time in thousands of years. In 1927 the first Jewish money was coined. Electricity was brought to the city of Jerusalem in 1929. By 1922 ninety-six percent of the Jews living in Israel claimed Hebrew as their mother tongue. It was the first time in history a "dead" language was revived to become the language of a living nation. On November 29, 1947, a resolution in the United Nations accepted the principle that two states should be established in Palestine. The state of Israel was called into being in Tel Aviv on May 14, 1948. Its first president was a Russian Jew, Chaim Weizmann, famous for discovering a method for producing acetone (an ingredient of TNT) from maize. Weizmann had given his discovery to the British government in exchange for Britain's promise that it would use its power to help the Jews secure a homeland in Palestine.

Many thousands of Jewish people moved to Palestine following the establishment of the state of Israel. Some estimates of the worldwide Jewish population indicate one-fifth is now found in Israel. Some Christians consider this to be the consummation of the Bible prophecy that a complete regathering of the Jews will occur prior to Christ's second coming. But it is inaccurate and reckless to say the existence of present-day Israel fulfills such prophecies. It is better described as a work of God to bring about conditions such as are to characterize the last days.

Joel and Ezekiel prophesy that the land will be inhabited by "the children of Zion" and "the house of Israel" at the time an invasion from the north takes place. Zechariah reveals that "the inhabitants of Jerusalem" will recognize their Messiah when he descends from heaven to deliver them. One-third of the people "in all the land" will be saved and become the Lord's people. Christ warns "them which be in Judaea" to flee when the abomination stands in the holy place. Both Daniel and Christ speak of the existence of a sacrificial system in Israel at the time of the Antichrist. Passages such as these do not explain how these large numbers of Jews happen to be in the land, but it is clear that the last days will find Palestine populated by Jewish people. Many of the same passages indicate the Jews will lack knowledge of the truth. They will have returned in a state of unbelief (Joel 2:17; Ezek. 39:22).

With the holy land occupied by the children of Israel for the first time in nearly two thousand years, the scene will be set for the unfolding of the events of the latter days. No one knows how long the Israeli nation may be in existence before those events begin to take place. Nevertheless, Bible students all over the world are convinced that conditions now exist such as the prophets described twenty-five hundred years ago, as they wrote about the time when God will intervene in the affairs of men.

In considerable detail, prophecy unfolds what lies ahead for the people of Israel. The next major occurrence will be the signing of a treaty between the people of Israel and "the prince that shall come," the Antichrist, the ruler of the western confederacy (Dan. 9:26, 27). This will mark the beginning of the final seven years. Daniel divides this period into two equal halves. The last half is properly called "the great tribulation" (Matt. 24:21).

During the first three and a half years the Jews will enjoy peace and prosperity, exciting the covetousness of a powerful nation in the north called "Rosh." The Jews will build a temple in Jerusalem and restore their ancient system of worship and sacrifices. Rosh will attempt to invade Israel, but will be destroyed by God. In the middle of these seven years the Antichrist will break his treaty, occupy the temple and demand worship, have an image installed, and begin the worst persecution of the Jews known to history. All the Jews in the land who know and believe Christ's warnings will flee. Two-thirds of the inhabitants will perish; one-third will become the people of God (Zech. 13:8, 9). Righteous Jews all over the world will experience the wrath of the devil (Rev. 12:17). Many will turn to the Lord (Deut. 30:2). Near the end of this period, all nations will invade Palestine, besieging and taking the city of Jerusalem (Zech. 14:2).

When this particular incident takes place, the hour for Christ's return will have arrived. The sky will cleave open and he will descend with the armies of heaven, saving Judah and Jerusalem before he puts an end to Armageddon (Zech. 12:7; Rev. 19:11-16). He will pour out his Spirit on those he came to save (Zech. 12:10), regather all Jews from the nations where they have been dispersed for so long, and establish his kingdom on earth.

Three times in their history it has been predicted the people of Israel would leave their land and later return to it. God said to Abram, "Know of a surety that thy seed shall be a stranger in a land that is not theirs, and shall serve them; and they shall afflict them four hundred years; and also that nation, whom they shall serve, will I judge: and afterward shall they come out with great substance" (Gen. 15:13, 14). This brief prophecy was fulfilled in the bondage in Egypt and the Exodus. A second departure took place when Nebuchadnezzar took the people captive to Babylon. "And this whole land shall . . . serve the king of Babylon seventy years. . . . For thus saith the Lord, That after seventy years be accomplished at Babylon I will visit you, and perform my good word toward you, in causing you to return to this place" (Jer. 25:11; 29:10). Nehemiah and Ezra describe the return.

The brevity of these predictions is striking in comparison with the innumerable prophecies of the present world dispersion and the ultimate regathering of the Jews. It is also noteworthy that the specific time of each of the first two absences was announced, while nothing is written about the number of years the Jewish people are to remain dispersed among all nations.

The first of many prophecies about the present scattering appears in Leviticus 26:33: "I will scatter you among the heathen" (see also Deut. 28:64; Jer. 9:16; Ezek. 12:15). Six books of the Bible contain such predictions. God said he would drive them out of their land, remove them, pluck them out, disperse them, and lead them captive. The time of this dispersion was placed after the destruction of the city of Jerusalem, which took place in A.D. 70 (Luke 21:20-24). Hosea reveals it will continue for many days and last until "the latter days" (see Hos. 3:2-5). It has already persisted for nearly two thousand years, and it will not end until the return of Christ to the earth.

The coming restoration of the Jews to their ancient homeland is mentioned more often than is the dispersion. It appears in thirteen books of the Bible. At least twelve different words are used to describe it. Thirty-five passages say God will gather the Jews. Another thirty-five texts say he will bring them back to their own land. Twenty-three passages say God is going to turn or bring back the captivity of Israel. It is said he will recover them, assemble them, lead them back, place them, take them, bring them, and plant them in their own land.

God says, "I will take you one of a city, and two of a family, and I will bring you to Zion" (Jer. 3:14). Some will come by themselves, one by one (Isa. 27:12). "I will send for many fishers, saith the Lord, and they shall fish them; and after will I send for many hunters, and they shall hunt them from every mountain, and from every hill, and out of the holes of the rocks" (Jer. 16:16). "Behold, I will bring them from the north country, and gather them from the coasts of the earth, and with them the blind and the lame, the woman with child and her that travaileth with child together: a great company shall return thither. They shall come with weeping, and with supplications will I lead them" (31:8, 9). Ships of Tarshish will bring them (Isa. 60:9), some will evidently come by plane (60:8). Every Jew in the world will be involved: "I have gathered them unto their own land, and have left none of them any more there" (Ezek. 39:28). They will never again leave Israel: "I will plant them upon their land, and they shall no more be pulled up out of their land which I have given them, saith the Lord thy God" (Amos 9:15).

The Jews are to be regathered after the return of Christ (Deut. 30:3; Matt. 24:31). Surprisingly, they are not to be regathered to the land, but to "the wilderness of the people," an expression most commentators apply to the Sinai peninsula (Ezek. 20:34-40). In that place the Lord will judge them and purge out the rebels, who "shall not enter into the land of Israel" (20:38). The righteous will then be restored to the land where they will serve the Lord God "in mine holy mountain, in the mountain of the height of Israel" (20:40).

This sampling of prophecy regarding the restoration of the Jews makes it clear that the world has not yet witnessed any of these things. God has certainly been at work in the present resettlement of Palestine, but all the Scripture passages which speak of the divine restoration still await fulfillment. The vision of the valley of dry bones, sometimes erroneously suggested as a prophecy of what is seen today, speaks of "the whole house of Israel," not a mere part of it (Ezek. 37:11).

After Christ has returned and regathered his people, he will remove the blindness divinely imposed on them (as prophesied in Isaiah 6:10; 29:10), which is still in effect during the present age (Rom. 11:7-25). All Israel will be saved. No unrighteous Jew will enter the kingdom (Jer. 23:6; Rom. 11:26). The Spirit will be poured out (Joel 2:28; Zech. 12:10). God will raise up David as king (Jer. 30:9). The ancient division of the twelve tribes into two kingdoms will be ended: "In those days the house of Judah shall walk with the house of Israel" (3:18; see also Ezek. 37:22). The people of Israel will be God's witnesses in the earth (Isa. 43:12). Men will call Jews "the Ministers of our God" (61:6).

"Ten men shall take hold out of all languages of the nations, even shall take hold of the skirt of him that is a Jew, saying, We will go with you: for we have heard that God is with you" (Zech. 8:23). It is written: "All the people of the earth . . . shall be afraid of [Israel]. . . . And the Lord shall make [Israel] the head, and not the tail" (Deut. 28:10, 13). Such passages are difficult for some to understand, but they are a part of the revelation given about the coming time when the oppressors of the Jews will discover that God is the God of Abraham, Isaac, and Jacob, whose descendants they have been persecuting. The Jews will be acknowledged among the Gentiles as enjoying the favor of God (Zech. 8:13). It will be discovered that God's blessings for the Gentiles come through the Jews, in accordance with God's promise to Abram (Gen. 12:3).

During the years of tribulation, the world population of Jews will be greatly reduced, but during the kingdom they are to become as populous as "the sand of the sea" (Hos. 1:10). Each individual will be able to expect a much longer life and will be free from the sicknesses and disabilities of the present age. God has promised to put a new spirit in them, "that they may walk in my statutes, and keep mine ordinances, and do them: and they shall be my people, and I will be their God" (Ezek. 11:20). They will be given "beauty for ashes, the oil of joy for mourning, the garment of praise for the spirit of heaviness" (Isa. 61:3). Israel will become fruitful for God in such a way as to benefit the entire world (27:6). The Jews will not be freed from the need for work. They will "build the old wastes," "raise up the former desolations," and "repair the waste cities" (61:4). They will have flocks, farms, and vineyards (61:5). Singing will be heard in the heights of Zion on the mountain of God (Jer. 31:12). Where they knew fear and trembling, there will be joy, songs, and dancing (31:13).

Scripture speaks of the future of the Jews as extending through the thousand-year reign of Messiah on earth, and throughout eternity. Israel's future is compared to that of the new heaven and the new earth which emerge in the final two chapters of the Book of Revelation: "As the new heavens and the new earth, which I will make, shall remain before me, saith the Lord, so shall your seed and your name remain" (Isa. 66:22). The eternal existence of the Jewish nation is likened to the never-ending laws God has ordained to govern the universe: "Thus saith the Lord, which giveth the sun for a light by day, and the ordinances of the moon and of the stars for a light by night, . . . if those ordinances depart from before me, saith the Lord, then the seed of Israel also shall cease from being a nation before me for ever" (Jer. 31:35, 36).

The people of God have looked forward for many centuries to the promised descent of the new Jerusalem from God out of heaven, set forth in some detail in Revelation 21. That description reveals that the names of the twelve tribes of the children of Israel will be found written on its twelve gates (Rev. 21:12). The church of Jesus Christ is to have its part in that heavenly city, but the Jewish people are to have a part as well. As the Bible comes to a close, they are still distinct from all other created beings who inhabit eternity. Abraham had some knowledge of these eternal events, because he "looked for a city . . . whose builder and maker is God" (Heb. 11:10). God had the Jews in mind from the beginning: "God is not ashamed to be called their God: for he hath prepared for them a city" (11:16).

One of Scripture's most profound statements is that God will dwell among men some day (Rev. 21:3). With that prospect in view, the children of Israel have been given the wonderful words, "The King of Israel, even the Lord, is in the midst of thee: thou shalt not see evil any more. . . . The Lord thy God in the midst of thee is mighty; he will save, he will rejoice over thee with joy; he will rest in his love, he will joy over thee with singing" (Zeph. 3:15, 17). The church is admonished to be glad and to rejoice over the coming marriage of the Lamb (Rev. 19:7), while Israel is given the picture of a singing God rejoicing over them throughout eternity after sorrow and sighing have fled away forever (Isa. 35:10).

CHAPTER 2
THE JEWS AND THE ARABS

The hatred of the Arab nations toward the people of Israel underlies much of the trouble in the Middle East. This enmity is anticipated in the Bible. There is also a considerable amount of prophecy about what will happen to some of the Arab nations in the day of the Lord. The word Arab does not appear in Scripture, nor are there predictions about Arabs as a people in the way we think of them today. Arabia is mentioned, however, as are the Arabians, who were the inhabitants of the world's largest peninsula during ancient times. Twelve of the modern Arab nations are located on or near the Arabian Peninsula.

The Arab peoples are all related by blood. The Muslim Arabs, like Mohammed, claim to have descended from Ishmael, Abraham's son by Hagar, and half brother to Isaac. Ishmael's mother was from Egypt, making him half Egyptian (Gen. 16:1-3, 15). Because he married a woman from the land of Egypt (21:21), his twelve children were three-quarters Egyptian. His daughter Mahalath became one of the wives of Esau (28:9). This linked Esau's descendants to Egypt as well. A number of Arab names are listed among the tribes which sprang from Ishmael. Among them are Kedar, Adbeel, and Dumah (25:13, 14).

It is prophesied about Ishmael that "he will be a wild man; his hand will be against every man, and every man's hand against him; and he shall dwell in the presence of all his brethren" (Gen. 16:12). Some versions translate this latter phrase to read that he would live in defiance of, or in hostility to, his brethren. There was apparently no open animosity between Isaac and Ishmael in their lifetimes, but history records the fulfillment of the prophecy in Ishmael's descendants. A recent newsmagazine article described the Arab nations as historically "brutal, ruthless, and viciously hostile" to the Jews.

Only two modern Arab nations bear ancient Bible names in our day: Syria and Egypt. Syria is mentioned scores of times in Scripture, but there is no specific prophecy relating it to the last days. Syria was the country to which Jacob fled for fear of his brother Esau; subsequently he was known as a Syrian (Hos. 12:12; Deut. 26:5). The apostle Paul ministered in Syria (Gal. 1:21). To learn what is to befall Syria in the end times, it is necessary to read about what will happen to "all the kingdoms of the world," or "the kings of the mingled people that dwell in the desert" in the great prophecy of Jeremiah 25:22-26.

Some nations from ancient times reappear in Scripture passages that deal with the future. Two such nations are Sheba and Dedan, located on the Arabian peninsula. Their ancestry is traced to two grandsons of Ham mentioned in Genesis 10:7, who occupied the region where Yemen is today, and to two grandsons of Abraham and Keturah who bore the same names and who also migrated to southern Arabia. Christ calls the queen of Sheba "the queen of the south" (Matt. 12:42). The name of Dedan may have been lent to an island existing today on the borders of the Persian Gulf; it is called Dadan.

The names "Sheba" and "Dedan" are given to two nations that will oppose the invasion of Israel by Rosh in the latter days (Ezek. 38:13). In the coming kingdom of Christ, Sheba will show forth the praises of the Lord (Isa. 60:6). The king of Sheba will offer gifts to the Messiah when he is reigning on the earth (Ps. 72:10). Dedan, on the other hand, is listed among the nations God is going to judge (Jer. 25:23). Tyre and Sidon appear in the same text.

Egypt is prominent not only in the history of ancient Israel, but in the end times as well. Of more than 750 references to Egypt (*Mizraim* in the Hebrew), more than fifty are prophetic.

Some think there may even be references to the present. Isaiah 19:7, 8 predicts the drying up of the reeds of the Nile, and the destruction of the river's fishing industry, where throughout history large quantities of fish have been taken with nets near its mouth. Both of these things began to take place after the construction of the Aswan Dam. Sediment which formerly nourished the country below the dam was trapped, thus depriving fish of nutrients needed to sustain life.

The closing three verses of Isaiah 19 present one of the most remarkable prophecies about Egypt's future: "In that day shall there be a highway out of Egypt to Assyria, and the Assyrian shall come into Egypt, and the Egyptian into Assyria, and the Egyptians shall serve with the Assyrians. In that day shall Israel be the third with Egypt and with Assyria, even a blessing in the midst of the land [earth]: whom the Lord of hosts shall bless, saying, " 'Blessed be Egypt my people, and Assyria the work of my hands, and Israel mine inheritance' " (Isa. 19:23-25).

The distance between Egypt and Assyria was approximately nine hundred miles. According to prophecy, the new highway will link the two nations located to the north and south of Israel. The river of Egypt, the Nile, marks the southwestern border of the land given to Abraham by God (Gen. 15:18). The language of Canaan will be spoken in cities of Egypt (Isa. 19:18). There, in the center of the world as it will be in the millennium, will stand three nations united in the blessing of the Lord.

Physical changes will take place in Egypt: "The Lord shall utterly destroy the tongue of the Egyptian sea" (Isa. 11:15), understood to be the Gulf of Suez. The difficult prophecy of Joel 3:19—"Egypt shall be a desolation"—which appears to refer to this same time, is evidently a parenthetic reference to the judgment which fell on Egypt in ancient times because of its mistreatment of the Jews. God made the land "desolate and waste" (Ezek. 29:9) while the Egyptian people were scattered and dispersed forty years, after which he brought the people back, to be "a base kingdom" (29:14).

An illuminating prophecy about Egypt is found in Zechariah 14:16-19. During the kingdom age, if a nation does not go up to Jerusalem to worship the King, the Lord of hosts, the rain will be withheld from that nation. If *Egypt* fails to go up to worship, however, it will be visited with the plague. This important passage shows not only that God will not hesitate to inflict disease on rebellious people during the millennium, but that during the kingdom Egypt will apparently not be dependent on rainfall, but will enjoy the historic blessing of the overflow of the Nile as it did throughout most of history. This seems to imply that the Aswan Dam will disappear during the great shaking of the earth at the time of Christ's return; the flow of the Nile once again will be uninterrupted.

There is more end-times prophecy about Edom than about any other Arab people. Edom was the name of the ancient nation that sprang from Esau (Gen. 36:1). Its land was also known as Mt. Seir, or Idumea, which meant "pertaining to Edom." The Edomites occupied the territory extending from the Dead Sea to the eastern part of the Arabian peninsula along the Persian Gulf. Arab names are found among the descendants of Esau, e.g., Omar, Elah, Kenaz (Gen. 36:15-43). The trouble between Jacob and Esau is familiar to every Bible student: "Esau hated Jacob because of the blessing wherewith his father blessed him: and Esau said in his heart, The days of mourning for my father are at hand; then will I slay my brother Jacob" (Gen. 27:41). This hatred was continued in intensified form by his posterity. The Edomites became inveterate enemies of the Jews. Saul had to fight them (1 Sam. 14:47), and they tried to invade Israel (2 Chron. 20:22). The Syrians of 2 Kings 16:16 are called Edomites in the Hebrew text. An Idumean, that is, an Edomite, son of Antipater, became Herod the Great, king of the Jews in 37 B.C. He was the king who sought to kill the child Jesus.

Scripture prophesies that Edom will face judgment in the day of the Lord. Ezekiel writes, "Because thou hast had a perpetual hatred, and hast shed the blood of the children of Israel by the force of the sword in the time of their calamity, . . . I will make thee perpetual desolation" (Ezek. 35:5, 9). Writes Joel, "Edom shall be a desolate wilderness, for the violence against the children of Judah, because they have shed innocent blood in their land" (Joel 3:19). This statement could easily refer to the terrorist acts against Jews during recent years.

The Book of Obadiah describes the future judgment of God on Edom. At the time of the exodus from Egypt, Edom was enjoying its golden age. Its capital was Bozrah, a city mentioned in connection with the return of Christ (Isa. 63:1). Obadiah recalls Edom's refusal to permit the Jews to pass through their land at the time of the exodus from Egypt (Num. 20:18), and refers to another occasion when Edom mistreated the children of Israel in the same way, evidently when they were being attacked and taken captive by Nebuchadnezzar.

The Edomites rejoiced over the calamity of the Jews. They helped in the sack of Jerusalem, captured as many of the fleeing people as they could, and turned them over to the enemy. Obadiah writes, "As thou hast done, it shall be done unto thee: thy reward shall return upon thine own head. . . . [T]here shall not be any remaining of the house of Esau; for the Lord hath spoken it" (Obad. 1:15, 18). When the kingdom of Christ is established on the earth, Edom will be gone forever, along with other Arab nations which have sought to destroy the chosen people of God.

CHAPTER 3
THE LAND OF ISRAEL

The Middle Eastern region formerly known as Palestine is the only land ever given by God to any nation. In a city called Ur in southern Babylonia, some four thousand years ago, the Lord spoke to Abram and told him to leave his own country and go to a land he had never seen. When Abram reached that place the Lord said, "Unto thy seed will I give this land" (Gen. 12:7). At that moment it became the promised land. From this point on, the Old Testament is devoted to the chosen people, their land, and the people who influenced them and their fortunes. A new divine program had been introduced. Through the descendants of Abram, God purposed to give to the world the Bible and the Savior of mankind.

Today that corner of the world has become a holy land for Christianity, Judaism, and Islam. It is revered by hundreds of millions of people. It forms a land bridge connecting the continents of Europe, Asia, and Africa. Most of the world's population is found on those three continents; the white, yellow, and black races meet in one geographic center. Their colors are blended in such a way that the native population is described as olive skinned. No race need feel excluded from the divine plan unfolding there.

This land, hereinafter called simply Israel, was ideally situated at the crossroads of ancient civilizations for the giving forth of God's message to the human race. It is the most strategically situated piece of real estate on earth, being located at the center of the land surface of the globe. It is called "the navel of the earth" in the original text of Ezekiel 38:12. A remarkable feature of the land is the Great Rift which runs north and south beneath the Jordan Valley. At the time of the return of Christ this ancient line of cleavage in the surface of the earth will be shaken by an earthquake which will change the face of the land.

Israel is referred to in the Old Testament fifteen hundred times. It is where the patriarchs lived, where David and Solomon reigned, where Christ walked, and where the church began. It is destined to become the scene of Armageddon, the last great war before the second coming of Christ. From that place he will rule the entire world from his throne in Jerusalem. The best descriptions of the land of Israel are to be found in the Bible. At the time the Jewish people were about to enter it under their great military genius, Joshua, they were told: "The Lord thy God bringeth thee into a good land, a land of brooks of water, of fountains and depths that spring out of valleys and hills; a land of wheat, and barley, and vines, and fig trees, and pomegranates; a land of oil olive, and honey; a land wherein thou shalt eat bread without scarceness, thou shalt not lack any thing in it; a land whose stones are iron, and out of whose hills thou mayest dig brass" (Deut. 8:7-9); and, "The land, whither ye go to possess it, is a land of hills and valleys, and drinketh water of the rain of heaven: a land which the Lord thy God careth for: the eyes of the Lord thy God are always upon it, from the beginning of the year even unto the end of the year" (11:11, 12).

Much can be discovered about Israel by studying the many names given to it in Scripture. It is the "land of Canaan" (Gen. 12:5), "the holy land" (Zech. 2:12), the "land of Jordan" (Ps. 42:6), the "glorious land" (Dan. 11:41), the "pleasant land" (Zech. 7:14), "an exceeding good land" (Num. 14:7), and "the glory of all lands' (Ezek. 20:6). Its most familiar designation, occurring some eighteen times, is "a land flowing with milk and honey" (Exod. 3:8). The Lord said, "the land is mine" (Lev. 25:23), and it is called "Jehovah's land" (Hos. 9:3, ASV). After God gave it to his chosen people, it became "the land of the Hebrews" (Gen. 40:15), "the land of Israel" (Matt. 2:20), and "the land of the Jews" (Acts 10:39).

God gave the boundaries of the land he promised to Abram "from the river of Egypt unto the great river, the river Euphrates" (Gen. 15:18). Many scholars believe the "river of Egypt" is the Nile, for the text uses the same word—*nahar*—of both the Euphrates and the river of Egypt, as is true elsewhere (2 Sam. 8:3; Isa. 19:5). Some confuse the river of Egypt with the Wady el-Arish, an intermittent stream, dry during the summer, located 140 miles northeast of the Nile. This mistake may arise from the fact that the Wady, incorrectly translated "river of Egypt" in Joshua 15:4, marked the southern border of the land actually occupied by the Jews under Joshua. The word for "Wady" is *nachal,* a ravine or narrow valley. It is often used of the brook Kidron (2 Sam. 15:23).

A remarkable parallel exists between the boundaries of the land given to Abram and the structure of the surface of the earth in that part of the world today. A fault line passes beneath the Persian Gulf and continues for eight hundred miles in a northwesterly direction beneath the river Euphrates, turning then toward the Mediterranean to meet the Great Rift, which extends from southeastern Africa through the Red Sea, and northward beneath the Jordan River basin. These fault lines, or fracture zones, are illustrated in the January 1973 issue of *National Geographic.* It shows that the entire Arabian Peninsula is set apart from the rest of the world as a distinct segment of the earth's surface. The land given by God to Abram is called the Arabian Plate, lying between the Eurasian and African Plates. It is surrounded by a great earthquake zone.

During the kingdom age, when the Jews possess all the land given to them by divine decree, they will evidently occupy all of the Arabian Peninsula. The "east sea" of Ezekiel 47:18 may be the Persian Gulf. The Red Sea is mentioned as one of the borders of the land: "I will set thy bounds from the Red sea even unto the sea of the Philistines" (Exod. 23:31). The Arabian Peninsula is the largest in the world. It is about one-third the size of the United States.

The fact that this great peninsula may become the future land of Israel casts light on what has always been considered to be a difficult text: "In that day shall there be a highway out of Egypt to Assyria. . . . In that day shall Israel be the third with Egypt and with Assyria, even a blessing in the midst of the land: whom the Lord of hosts shall bless, saying, Blessed be Egypt my people, and Assyria the work of my hands, and Israel mine inheritance" (Isa. 19:23-25). The Euphrates will be the border between Israel and Assyria, and the Nile will form the border with Egypt. The two countries will adjoin Israel in the kingdom age.

This land is frequently mentioned in the Bible as the inheritance of the people of Israel (Deut. 19:10). It has always been to the Jews "the land which the Lord thy God giveth thee for an inheritance to possess it" (Deut. 15:4). It was the first land of freedom known to history. America took a text of Scripture containing a message for the land of the Jews and inscribed it on the Liberty Bell: "Proclaim liberty throughout all the land unto all the inhabitants thereof" (Lev. 25:10). Although some have insisted that Israel and the church are synonymous, the Jews have always been inseparably connected with the land. This land is never mentioned in the church epistles except as the place where Abraham sojourned (Heb. 11:9). Our inheritance is reserved in heaven (1 Pet. 1:4). When the Lord returns to receive his church, he will not come to the land, but to the air.

The blessing of God on the land has always been linked to the obedience of his chosen people. He said to them, "If ye walk in my statutes, and keep my commandments, and do them; then I will give you rain in due season, and the land shall yield her increase, and the trees of the field shall yield their fruit" (Lev. 26:3, 4).

Such blessings were to end and be replaced by a curse if the people were disobedient: "If ye will not hearken unto me, and will not do all these commandments; . . . I will bring the land into desolation" (Lev. 26:14, 32); "If thou wilt not hearken unto the voice of the Lord thy God, to observe to do all his commandments and his statutes which I command thee this day; . . . all these curses shall come upon thee, and overtake thee. . . . And thy heaven that is over thy head shall be brass, and the earth that is under thee shall be iron. The Lord shall make the rain of thy land powder and dust . . . until thou be destroyed" (Deut. 28:15, 23, 24).

The Old Testament stands as a record of the tragic failure of the people of Israel. Their sin is the cause for what happened to the land: "I will make the land desolate, because they have committed a trespass, saith the Lord God" (Ezek. 15:8); "The land shall be desolate because of them that dwell therein, for the fruit of their doings" (Mic. 7:13); "The land is full of adulterers; for because of swearing the land mourneth; the pleasant places of the wilderness are dried up" (Jer. 23:10). God warned the Jews against the practice of the abominations they had learned from the pagan nations whom he had driven out of Canaan, "that the land spue not you out also, when ye defile it, as it spued out the nations that were before you" (Lev. 18:28). The warning was fulfilled. The people were cast out and scattered, leaving behind what became a deserted, barren waste.

The question is asked, "[Why was] the land . . . burned up like a wilderness?"; the Lord answers: "Because they have forsaken my law which I set before them, and have not obeyed my voice" (Jer. 9:12, 13); "Thou hast polluted the land . . . with thy wickedness. . . . Therefore the showers have been withholden, and there hath been no latter rain" (3:2, 3). Locusts destroyed the vegetation that still grew; worms ate the grapes of the vineyards; olive trees cast their fruit (Deut. 28:38-40). Fields that had been fertile brought forth thorns and briers (Isa. 32:13). The land became "a desolation, and an astonishment, and a curse" (Jer. 44:22). And after everything was consumed, famine was the result (Zeph. 1:2; Ezek. 14:13).

All of this took place thousands of years ago. Today the land contains a Jewish population again. Once more there is an Israeli nation prospering there.

Barren desert places have become rich and productive because of Israeli genius and hard work. This has been widely acclaimed as a fulfillment of prophecy, but passages of Scripture quoted as proof are largely misapplied. Guides point to lush vegetation and rich produce and say, "The desert is blossoming as the rose, as prophesied in Isaiah 35:1," but they say nothing about the following verses. The eyes of the blind are not yet opened, nor are the ears of the deaf unstopped. Isaiah was actually writing about conditions as they will be after the Lord has returned and established his kingdom.

God is going to regather his ancient people and restore them to their land, but this will not take place until after the Lord has returned to the earth (Deut. 30:3; Matt. 24:31). The promised regathering is to be done by angels, in a miraculous fashion (Jer. 16:14-18), and it will involve every Jew on earth (Ezek. 39:28). To say, as some do, that the recent increase in rainfall fulfills Joel's prophecy, "He will cause to come down from you the rain" (Joel 2:23), is to overlook the context which speaks of a time after the Jews have been supernaturally delivered from an invasion of armies from the north. It is not accurate to say we have seen the fulfillment of the words, "This land that was desolate is become like the garden of Eden" (Ezek. 36:35), because the passage describes conditions as they are going to be after the Lord has come and cleansed Israel from her iniquities.

A bus-load of American tourists was recently visiting Israel. One man complained that the country, far from being a place flowing with milk and honey as the Bible describes it, was a burning desert of stones and barrenness. A Christian in the group opened his Bible and said, "You have just fulfilled a prophecy found in the same book you have criticized." He read the words, "The generation to come . . . and the stranger that shall come from a far land, shall say, when they shall see the plagues of that land, and the sicknesses which the Lord hath laid upon it; and that the whole land thereof is brimstone, and salt, and burning, that it is not sown, nor beareth, nor any grass groweth therein, . . . Even all nations shall say, Wherefore hath the Lord done thus unto this land?" (Deut. 29:22-24).

I once had an experience in Jerusalem that illustrates the widespread interest in finding possible fulfillments of prophecy. A young Jewish guide asked me, "Did you know the Bible predicted modern archaeology?" To prove his point he turned to Psalm 102:13, 14 and read, "Thou shalt arise, and have mercy upon Zion: for the time to favour her, yea, the set time, is come. For thy servants take pleasure in her stones, and favour the dust thereof." He concluded, "This is precisely what the archaeologists are doing. They are delighted with the old stones they dig up, they carefully screen the dust to find artifacts." That young man had a better case for his claim than most people do who are eager to claim prophecy is being fulfilled.

The Lord has a vested interest in the land of Israel. He cares for it and his eyes are continually on it. In the latter days when a great pagan host invades it and begins to devastate it, he will say, "Fear not, O land; be glad and rejoice: for the Lord will do great things" (Joel 2:21). He has said in the past when enemies have hurt it, "They have made it desolate, and being desolate it mourneth unto me" (Jer. 12:11). This is echoed in the New Testament: "For we know that the whole creation groaneth and travaileth in pain together until now" (Rom. 8:22).

After the present age has ended, Israel will become the scene of divine activity and the center of world attention. The God who said, "I will bring the land into desolation" (Lev. 26:32) also said, "I will remember the land" (26:42). He "will be merciful unto his land, and to his people" (Deut. 32:43). At the beginning of the final seven years before the Lord's return, the land will be populated by Jewish people in such large numbers they will be able to sign a treaty with the Antichrist. There will be a temple in Jerusalem, and the ancient sacrificial system will be restored. The Jews will enjoy peace and security, but they will reject the Christian teaching that the Messiah whom they await is Jesus of Nazareth (Matt. 24:15; Zech. 12:10).

At some time during those last days, "the prince of Rosh" will lead a northern confederacy against the land, provoking the wrath of God. The Lord will destroy the invading forces by using the same weapons anciently employed against Israel's enemies. An earthquake will shake the land and the confused armies will begin to destroy each other. Pestilence will decimate their ranks. Great hail, fire, and brimstone will fall from the sky. God will intervene in such a way as to astonish the world (Ezek. 38, 39). Many students believe this will provide the opportunity for the Antichrist to become a world ruler—his greatest enemy, the Soviet Union, will have been removed from the scene.

Severe persecution in those days will drive many Jews from the land. The Antichrist will stop the temple worship, sit in the temple as a god, have an image placed there for all to worship. The city of Jerusalem will come under Gentile control for three and a half years. The land will witness wonderful and dreadful events. For example, God will send two witnesses who will call down fire from heaven as in the days of Elijah. When these divine representatives are killed, the land will become the focal point of world attention. The armies of all nations ultimately will gather at Armageddon, the plain of Esdraelon, east of Mt. Carmel.

In the midst of that great conflagration, the city of Jerusalem will be surrounded and taken by attacking forces. Suddenly the sky above the city will open and every eye will see Israel's Messiah descending with the armies of heaven. As his feet touch the earth at the Mount of Olives, five physical changes will take place, as described by the prophet Zechariah: (1) a great earthquake will shake the land; (2) the Mount of Olives will split open, creating a tremendous valley that will extend eastward from the city; (3) the entire area will be leveled, producing a plain extending north and south from Jerusalem for a total of thirty-five miles; (4) the city itself will be thrust upward, so that it dominates the countryside from a high mountain during the kingdom age; and (5) a river will spring up from beneath the surface of the earth, flowing westward into the Mediterranean and eastward into the Jordan valley (Zech. 14:4-10).

Other great changes are to take place. At the same time that the land becomes a plain, the entire Jordan valley, including the sea of Galilee, will be lifted to sea level. The millennial river and the Jordan will flow into the Dead Sea at the same level as the Mediterranean and the Gulf of Aqaba. The hot and sultry climate of the Jordan valley will be a thing of the past. A number of references to mountains indicate that the land will still contain a considerable area of mountainous terrain. It is mentioned incidentally that there will be a new fishing industry near En-Gedi (Ezek. 47:10). There will still be a region given to salt near the Dead Sea; thus the flooding of the basin with fresh water will not put an end to the obtainment of wealth from the accumulated deposits of many centuries in that region (47:11).

During the kingdom age streams will flow down from the highlands (Isa. 41:18) and broad rivers will be found everywhere (33:21). Some of these will necessarily empty into the Mediterranean, breaking up the smooth coast with numerous inlets and harbors (the only good harbor in the present age is at Haifa, near the foot of Mt. Carmel). Scattered everywhere will be populous cities. The "wastes shall be builded" and the "desolate land shall be tilled" (Ezek. 36:33, 34) so that farms and vineyards will be seen where deserts are found today. "They shall say, this land that was desolate is become like the garden of Eden" (36:35).

Along the Mediterranean coast the twelve tribes of Israel will occupy parallel strips of land extending eastward from the sea to the Jordan valley, each strip twenty-five miles wide. Ezekiel 48 gives the order of the tribes from north to south as Dan, Asher, Naphtali, Manasseh, Ephraim, Reuben, and Judah. Below Judah comes an area called "the holy oblation," given to the priests and Levites for the service of the temple.

South of this will be a strip of land about twelve and a half miles wide, extending from the Mediterranean to the Jordan. This strip will be set apart for the city of Jerusalem with its gardens and suburbs.

The city will lie on the southern slope of the great mountain of God, below the peak on which the temple will stand, overlooking the millennial river on the south. The city is described as situated "on the sides of the north" (Ps. 48:2). This seems to refer to the sides of the mountain or highland rising to the north of the river, which divides the land of Israel into northern and southern parts. South of the river the remaining five tribes (Benjamin, Simeon, Issachar, Zebulun, and Gad) will occupy strips of territory like those of the northern tribes.

Jerusalem is to be the capital city of the world during the kingdom. Occupying the throne of David will be the Lord Jesus Christ. From year to year the Gentiles will go up to Jerusalem to worship the King, the Lord of hosts, and to learn the law of the Lord (Isa. 2:1-4; Zech. 14:16).

The brief descriptions found in Scripture provide a faint idea of the beauty of the place. Towers and palaces will rise above the walls surrounding the city, shining in the sun, high above the wide plain below. Crystal waters will flow down over the terraces of the mountain of God, clothed in trees and flowers planted by the Lord to beautify the place of his sanctuary (Isa. 60:13, 14).

At the crest of the mountain will stand the temple of the Lord, about twelve miles north of the city proper. It will be built in the center of a court one mile square, with a smaller court inside. Ezekiel describes the temple and its surroundings in the last chapters of his prophecy. From the east side of the temple threshold will flow a stream of water which grows larger as it flows, being joined by other streams, eventually becoming the great millennial river.

Crowning the mountain of God like a canopy will be "a cloud and smoke by day, and the shining of a flaming fire by night" (Isa. 4:5). Isaiah's revelation is so brief and challenging that commentators can only compare it to the pillar of cloud and of fire that guided the children of Israel when they wandered through the wilderness (Exod. 13:21). Psalm 48, beloved by the people of God for centuries, accurately describes what Jerusalem will look like when that city has become the world capital. It will be "beautiful for situation, the joy of the whole earth" (Ps. 48:2). From the windows of heaven God will pour out a blessing "that there shall not be room enough to receive it" (Mal. 3:10). All nations will call Israel blessed, and the final promise of God concerning the place he gave to Abraham long ago will be fulfilled, "for ye shall be a delightsome land, saith the Lord of hosts" (3:12).

CHAPTER 4
THE FUTURE WORLD CAPITAL

The Bible tells us that Jerusalem will become the world's chief metropolis during the reign of the Messiah in the kingdom age. It is to be the most strategically situated city on earth, the place of the throne of the Lord, beautiful beyond compare. It will be the center of world worship, canopied with the glory of God visible in a cloud by day and in fire by night.

In God's plan, Jerusalem has always been the most important city on earth. The Bible mentions it nearly twelve hundred times, and many of these references are prophetic. Jerusalem is given a variety of names and descriptive titles. At least thirty of them appear in the prophecy of Isaiah alone, where it is called the "city of David," the "holy city," the "city of righteousness," and the "Zion of the Holy One of Israel."

In Jerusalem the prophets spoke, David and Solomon reigned, and the Shekinah glory appeared in the temple. There Christ taught and was crucified, buried, and resurrected. From its Mount of Olives he ascended, and to that place he will return again. The age of the church began there nearly two thousand years ago when the Holy Spirit descended from heaven on the day of Pentecost.

The ancient capital of Israel has influenced world history more than any other city, in spite of its small size and remote location. It has always been far removed from main routes of commerce, having no river or port, and being isolated by mountains and deserts. Many of the great cities of ancient times declined and died and were forgotten for so long that their ruins were lost for centuries, leading scholars to conclude they never even existed. Yet Jerusalem has undergone at least twenty-seven sieges and has been captured, destroyed, ploughed like a field, and forsaken, only to rise again and again from its ashes.

The prophet Ezekiel made two striking statements regarding the uniqueness of Jerusalem's geographical location. He wrote, "Thus saith the Lord God; This is Jerusalem: I have set it in the midst of the nations and countries that are round about her" (Ezek. 5:5); the people of Israel were said to dwell "in the navel of the earth" (38:12, lit.). A look at any world map confirms this divine revelation. The city is indeed located at the center of the earth's land mass.

> As the navel is set in the center of the human body, so is the land of Israel the navel of the world . . . situated in the center of the world, and Jerusalem in the center of the land of Israel, and the sanctuary in the center of Jerusalem, and the holy place in the center of the sanctuary, and the ark in the center of the holy place. (The Midrash)

The key to the location of Jerusalem in such a remarkable spot is found in Psalm 132:13: "The Lord hath chosen Zion; he hath desired it for his habitation." (The Bible often refers to Jerusalem as "Zion.") Not only did God choose it, but "the Lord hath founded Zion" (Isa. 14:32). In the latter days he will choose it again (Zech. 1:17; 2:12). He purposes to make it the center of his future plan for the world and its people.

The first time Jerusalem appears in Scripture it is given its ancient name of Salem (Gen. 14:18; cf. Ps. 76:1, 2). A confederacy of Gentile nations had invaded the land of Israel. They took captives and seemed to be victorious. Then God intervened, gave a great victory to Abraham and his people, and delivered them from their enemies. Melchizedek, king of Salem, suddenly dominated the scene. His name means king of righteousness, and he was also "king of peace" (the literal translation of the Hebrew word *Salem*). This mysterious ruler of Jerusalem blessed Abraham and received tithes from him. Then Melchizedek brought out bread and wine, the elements used today in the Lord's Supper. Abraham said afterward, "I have lift up mine hand unto the Lord, the most high God, the possessor of heaven and earth" (Gen. 14:22).

Here for a brief moment we see Jerusalem as it is going to be in the last days. Its ruler will be the Lord Jesus Christ, King of Righteousness and King of Peace (Heb. 7:1-21). He will appear on the scene after Jerusalem has been attacked by all the nations of the earth (Zech. 14:1-3). During Israel's darkest hour the city will fall, and half its people will be taken captive. Suddenly the Lord will descend from heaven, deliver the Jews by vanquishing their foes, establish his kingdom, and rule the world from Jerusalem as his world capital. Like Melchizedek, Christ will bless his people. The kings of the earth will bring gifts to him (Ps. 72:10).

The rich and tragic history of Jerusalem is presented in Scripture, covering a period of four thousand years. This record is the historical and prophetic background for the final glorious destiny of Jerusalem. The end of Gentile world government is linked to the city. "Jerusalem shall be trodden down of the Gentiles, until the times of the Gentiles be fulfilled" (Luke 21:24). Some believe that Gentile times were "fulfilled" when Israel took control of the city in 1967 for the first time in over two thousand years. This interpretation is based on the use of a similar expression by Christ when he said, "The time is fulfilled, and the kingdom of God is at hand" (Mark 1:15). If this is so, then present world conditions are the first birth-pangs of a new age, and Gentile world rule is nearing its end. Whatever the true meaning of our Lord's words may be, the ancient capital of Israel is to be the center of the stage as the old order winds down and the city of God emerges to dominate the new order. The seizure of the ancient walled city by the new nation of Israel in 1967 may have been the first act in a developing drama which will prepare Jerusalem for the return of the Messiah.

Scripture says that in the latter days Jerusalem will become a source of international trouble. God "will make Jerusalem a cup of trembling unto all the prople round about. . . . [I]n that day will I make Jerusalem a burdensome stone for all people" (Zech. 12:2, 3). This revelation introduces Jerusalem's terrible final days and the glorious destiny to follow. Zechariah declares, "Behold, the day of the Lord cometh, and thy spoil shall be divided in the midst of thee. For I will gather all nations against Jerusalem to battle; and the city shall be taken, and the houses rifled, and the women ravished; and half the city shall go forth into captivity, and the residue of the people shall not be cut off from the city. Then shall the Lord go forth, and fight against those nations, as when he fought in the day of battle" (14:1-3).

This scene will take place at the end of what is commonly called the battle of Armageddon, when the spirits of demons "go forth unto the kings of the earth and of the whole world, to gather them to the battle of that great day of God Almighty" (Rev. 16:14). Demons will move the nations to unite in battle; but behind the scenes God will be working to bring about the fulfillment of prophecy.

The prophecy of Zechariah 14 provides a panorama of the events that will take place at Jerusalem as it changes from an embattled and defeated city to become the capital of the world. The record begins with a dark picture of the city surrounded by armies. The houses are rifled, women are mistreated, and half of the population is taken captive. These are the circumstances which indicate the imminence of Christ's second coming.

"Then shall the Lord go forth, and fight against those nations, as when he fought in the day of battle (Zech. 14:3). One such "day of battle" was when the captain of the host of the Lord came to help the armies of Israel in their conquest of Canaan (Josh. 5:14). The Lord Jesus Christ has always been recognized as this captain. When heaven opens and the Lord returns to deliver Jerusalem and to bring an end to Armageddon, he will be accompanied by the armies of heaven (Rev.

19:11-14). All the saints are to be with him (Zech. 14:5). The raptured church will be present, because Christians are forever to be with the Lord.

When the Lord will reappear was also revealed to Zechariah, a revelation confirmed in the statement made to the disciples at the time of Christ's ascension. They were told he would return "in like manner" as he ascended to heaven from the Mount of Olives (Acts 1:11). After the Lord goes forth from heaven to deliver his embattled people, "his feet shall stand in that day upon the mount of Olives, which is before Jerusalem on the east" (Zech. 14:4). Why are his feet mentioned? Why does the text not simply say he will stand on the mount? One possible explanation is that this is the moment when the people of Israel will look on him whom they have pierced, recognizing by his pierced feet that he is the Messiah they rejected at his first coming (12:10). The great mourning in Jerusalem on that occasion will afterward give way to rejoicing: "Joy and gladness shall be found therein, thanksgiving, and the voice of melody" (Isa. 51:3).

As his feet stand on the Mount of Olives on that day, the effect will be like that of a great earthquake. "The mount of Olives shall cleave in the midst thereof toward the east and toward the west, and there shall be a very great valley; and half of the mountain shall remove toward the north, and half of it toward the south" (Zech. 14:4). This coincides with what is written in Revelation 16:18 about "a great earthquake, such as was not since men were upon the earth, so mighty an earthquake, and so great."

Visitors to Israel today are told that building operations on the Mount of Olives are forbidden because of the danger of earthquakes. Geologists have discovered a line of cleavage in the earth's crust passing directly through it from east to west. This cleft is actually visible as one looks at the mount from the city. There is a notch opposite the Golden Gate where a walled roadway follows what is believed to be the ancient fault line.

One wonders whether Zechariah may not have been describing a *literal* fulfillment of Christ's reference to faith so great "ye shall say unto this mountain, Remove hence to yonder place, and it shall remove" (Matt. 17:20). God's people are going to "do exploits" (Dan. 11:32). Saints in Jerusalem, knowing of this prophecy in Zechariah, may call upon the Lord to deliver them by opening a miraculous way of escape. A similar prayer is recorded in Isaiah 64:1: "Oh that thou wouldest rend the heavens, that thou wouldest come down, that the mountains might flow down at thy presence."

When Olivet splits open "there shall be a very great valley" (Zech. 14:4). The word used by Zechariah describes a deep place with lofty sides. Joel describes the valley of Jehoshaphat by using a word meaning "broad and spacious," where the Lord is to judge the nations gathered against Jerusalem. Both references appear to speak of the same place, a valley not yet in existence. Guides in Palestine point to the small depression between Jerusalem and the Mount of Olives called the valley of the Kidron, and say that is where Christ will judge the nations. However, there is no biblical basis for such a notion. Kidron was never called Jehoshaphat until some time during the fourth century.

The inhabitants of Jerusalem will flee through this newly-created escape route, just as their ancestors fled from a great earthquake in the days of Uzziah. The valley will "reach unto Azal" (Zech. 14:5), a place no one can locate with certainty. Some scholars have assumed it will be near Jerusalem, others have placed it on the shore of the Mediterranean. It has also been suggested that Azal refers to the deep valley extending for one hundred miles from the Dead Sea to the Gulf of Aqaba; it is destined to form the channel for a great river during the kingdom age.

"And it shall be in that day, that living waters shall go out from Jerusalem; half of them toward the former sea, and half of them toward the hinder sea: in summer and in winter shall it be" (Zech. 14:8). These "living," or flowing, waters describe the millennial river which is to flow from Jerusalem westward into the Mediterranean Sea and eastward into the Dead Sea when Christ reigns as King. Four different Hebrew terms for "this river" appear in Scripture. Zechariah used the word *mayim,* meaning "flowing waters." Joel calls it a *mahyon,* a "fountain or spring rising from a subterranean source": "a fountain shall come forth of the house of the Lord, and shall water the valley of Shittim," near the Dead Sea (Joel 3:18). The psalmist used *nachal,* the common word for rivers such as the Nile, when he wrote, "There is a river, the streams whereof shall make glad the city of God, the holy place of the tabernacles of the Most High" (Ps. 46:4).

The longest description of this future stream appears in Ezekiel 47. The prophet uses the word *nahar,* which refers to the Euphrates in several passages (2 Kings 23:29). Both Ezekiel and Joel say the source of these waters will be the temple of God. In his vision Ezekiel saw the waters flowing from the east side of the temple, past the altar, and out the east gate of the temple court. As he was taken eastward through the waters for a distance of over a mile, he found that they gradually increased in depth until they became "a river that I could not pass over: for the waters were risen, waters to swim in, a river that could not be passed over" (Ezek. 47:5). Great trees grew on its banks, unlike any seen on earth today.

Zechariah informs us that half of the waters will go from Jerusalem toward the former (the Dead Sea) and half of them will flow toward the hinder sea (the Mediterranean). They will descend eastward into what is now a desert. When this fresh water reaches the Dead Sea, its salt waters will be "healed," or made fresh, supporting a fishing industry where none could exist today. Ezekiel's word for desert is *arabah,* used to describe the valley lying between Mount Hermon and the Dead Sea, particularly that part of it which forms the lowest valley on the face of the earth. This valley connects the Dead Sea basin with the Gulf of Aqaba and the Red Sea.

Several details of this revelation make it clear that the millennial river will be navigable. Ezekiel speaks of its depth and the transformation it will bring to the salt waters of the Dead Sea, which the Jordan and other rivers have not been able to accomplish. He also refers to a "mighty river," such as the Euphrates. There are several other Old Testament references to other flowing streams which, because of the topography of the land, will augment the size of the main river: "There shall be upon every high mountain, and upon every high hill, rivers and streams of waters" (Isa. 30:25); "I will open rivers in high places, and fountains in the midst of the valleys" (41:18). One of these passages contains a curious statement: "The glorious Lord will be unto us a place of broad rivers and streams; wherein shall go no galley with oars, neither shall gallant ship pass thereby" (33:21). Scholars understand that these unusual Hebrew words refer only to *hostile* ships of war, implying that other shipping will indeed pass Jerusalem in that era of peace on earth when Christ reigns.

The existence of such a great waterway entirely within Israel will make Jerusalem the most strategic spot on the face of the earth. It will be situated at the geographical center where the continents of Europe, Asia, and Africa meet. Connecting the Mediterranean with the Jordan Valley, this great fresh water system will make the Dead Sea the finest inland port in the world. All the ships of all nations could conceivably find anchorage in the Dead Sea, which will then be at sea level. Ships moving between the Mediterranean Sea and the Indian Ocean will have to pass through it, because the Suez Canal will no longer exist after the convulsions which change the earth at the second coming of Christ: "The Lord shall utterly destroy the tongue of the Egyptian Sea" (Isa. 11:15)—For centuries, students have understood this to be a reference to the Gulf of Suez. Without the gulf, the canal could not exist.

Zechariah gives us a remarkable detail about the area of Israel adjacent to Jerusalem during the millennium: "All the land shall be turned like a plain from Geba to Rimmon south of Jerusalem" (Zech. 14:10). This is in agreement with Isaiah 54:10: "The mountains shall depart, and the hills be removed." A large part of the Holy Land now covered with steep hills and deep valleys will become level as a plain when God "ariseth to shake terribly the earth" (2:19). Geba is six miles north of

Jerusalem; Rimmon is thirty miles south. The land will be approximately sixty miles wide at this point. The level plain will cover 2,160 square miles.

The most striking change in the land will be the creation of a high mountain where Jerusalem is to be located: "Jerusalem . . . shall be lifted up, and inhabited in her place" (Zech. 14:10). While Zechariah briefly describes the tremendous upheaval which will lift the city far above the countryside, at least twenty-two other references, by eight different prophets, speak of Jerusalem as located on a mountain during the millennium. Best known of these is Isaiah 2:2-4: "And it shall come to pass in the last days, that the mountain of the Lord's house shall be established in the top of the mountains, and shall be exalted above the hills; and all nations shall flow into it. And many people shall go and say, Come ye, and let us go up to the mountain of the Lord, to the house of the God of Jacob; and he will teach us of his ways, and we will walk in his paths: for out of Zion shall go forth the law, and the word of the Lord from Jerusalem." Some commentators have assumed that these words cannot be understood literally; they have interpreted this passage as a reference to the exalted character of the throne of the Lord. But too much has been revealed about the future of Jerusalem to make such a view tenable.

Ezekiel informs us that a divine messenger brought him into the land of Israel, and set him on a very high mountain, where he saw a structure like a city on the south (Ezek. 40:2). He ends his prophecy with these words: "and the name of the city from that day shall be, The Lord is there" (48:35). In between these passages he describes what the Lord calls "my holy mountain Jerusalem" (Isa. 66:20): "the place of my throne, and the place of the soles of my feet" (Ezek. 43:7). Fourteen times the prophet speaks of the mountaintop city which he saw in his vision.

The exact location of Jerusalem during the kingdom age is revealed to us in plain language. Zechariah reveals that it will be "inhabited in her place" (Zech. 14:10), and Jeremiah wrote, "the city shall be builded upon her own heap" (Jer. 30:18). The Hebrew word for "heap" is *tel*, a mound formed by debris resulting from the destruction and rebuilding of a city many times during an extended period of years. Archaeologists exploring tels today find one layer of occupation after another, often to a great depth. Jerusalem itself is built on a tel where the debris is nearly one hundred feet deep in some places, resulting from the repeated leveling of earlier cities over a four-thousand-year period.

Shifts in the surface of the land during the upheavals accompanying the return of the Lord will not alter the revealed fact that the millennial city is to stand where Jerusalem now stands. Measurements and other data based on information recorded by Ezekiel support this fact.

One of the most beautiful descriptions of the millennial city is found in Psalm 48:1, 2: "Great is the Lord, and greatly to be praised in the city of our God, in the mountain of his holiness. Beautiful for situation, the joy of the whole earth, is mount Zion, on the sides of the north, the city of the great King." The Hebrew word rendered "situation" is better translated "elevation." It is a word picture of a mountain, not rugged or precipitous, but rising in graceful, wavelike terraces. Isaiah wrote of it when he said, "The glory of Lebanon shall come unto thee, the fir tree, the pine tree, and the box together, to beautify the place of my sanctuary; and I will make the place of my feet glorious" (Isa. 60:13), and "Instead of the thorn shall come up the fir tree, and instead of the brier shall come up the myrtle tree" (55:13). Vegetation will grow on that mountain such as has never been seen since the beginning of the curse (Gen. 3:17, 18).

The city of the great King is to be located "on the sides of the north" (Ps. 48:2). This ancient expression refers to the slopes of the mountain of God which stand on the north side of the millennial river. The mountain will mark the southern border of the northern part of Israel, a nation divided into two parts by the river during the kingdom age.

If the measurements of the city given in Ezekiel 48 are

translated into miles, we find the city is to be twelve miles square. It will be surrounded by walls, with three gates on each side, named for the twelve tribes of Israel (Ezek. 48:31-34). The total area will be 144 square miles. On either side of the city proper will be twelve miles of gardens; these gardens will be a main source of food (48:18). Within the walls, old men and women will watch boys and girls playing on wide "streets," which are literally broad places or parks (Zech. 8:4, 5). It will be a holy city (Joel 3:17) and a city of truth (Zech. 8:3), in striking contrast with metropolitan centers today.

One final revelation has been given about that future city: "The Lord will create upon every dwelling place of mount Zion, and upon her assemblies, a cloud and smoke by day, and the shining of a flaming fire by night: for upon all the glory shall be a [canopy, lit.]" (Isa. 4:5). This is remarkably similar to the pillar of cloud and fire which manifested the presence of Israel's God in the wilderness long ago (Exod. 13:21). During those early days in Israel's history, the glory of the Lord appeared in the cloud (16:10). It was like a devouring fire (24:17), and like a rainbow (Ezek. 1:28). When it filled the house of God in the days of Solomon, "the priests could not stand to minister by reason of the cloud" (2 Chron. 5:14).

God has promised, "I will glorify the house of my glory" in that coming day (Isa. 60:7). The house of his glory will be the millennial temple, described in detail in the closing chapters of Ezekiel. The temple will stand within the great sanctuary at the crest of the mountain north of the city proper (Ezek. 43:12). From it will flow the waters of Ezekiel's vision, pouring out from the east side (47:1, 2).

Ezekiel provides us with so many particulars and details about the sanctuary and the temple that architects have been able to determine that such a place could conceivably be constructed today. Models of the temple have been prepared, and photographs of them are to be found in certain Bible commentaries.

Above the beautiful towers and palaces of the millennial city the glory of God will shine. This prospect has found its way into Jewish custom. Every time a couple unites in marriage beneath a wedding canopy, they unwittingly portray the covering presence of the Lord seen in the ancient pillar of cloud and of fire, and in the future canopy of glory which will mark the location of Jerusalem during the millennium. As the bridegroom rejoices over his bride, so will God rejoice over his people when they have finally entered into their rest, and when Jerusalem has become the joy of the whole earth.

The prophetic theme of Jerusalem's future glory seems to have little practical value to Christians today. But that glorious place of shining palaces and turrets, high up on a mountain and overshadowed by the glory of God, will play an important part in the destiny of every believer.

Christ promised that we shall be with him forever and that we shall reign with him on the earth. He has made it very clear that we are to sit with him on his throne (Rev. 3:21). The throne is to be at Jerusalem: "At that time they shall call Jerusalem the throne of the Lord" (Jer. 3:17), the holy mountain of God (Isa. 66:20). Attempts to claim that such statements cannot be literal are nullified by words like those of the Lord, to be uttered after he enters his millennial temple at the crest of a very high mountain. The Lord will call his temple "the place of my throne, and the place of the soles of my feet, where I will dwell in the midst of the children of Israel for ever" (Ezek. 43:7).

There has always been a present aspect to what has been revealed about the holy city of God. Christians have long rejoiced over the promise of Psalm 122:6: "Pray for the peace of Jerusalem: they shall prosper that love thee." These words have been compared with Genesis 12:3: "I will bless them that bless thee." Over the centuries believers have treasured the promises associated with loving the capital city of Israel and blessing God's ancient people.

CHAPTER 5
JOEL'S OUTLINE
OF FUTURE EVENTS

The Book of Joel appears to be insignificant—it contains a mere three chapters. Yet Joel is the book from which the apostle Peter chose the text for his sermon on the day of Pentecost. Joel's prophecy provides an incomparable outline of coming events. At its heart is one of Scripture's most remarkable revelations for God's people. It contains a famous gospel message quoted in the New Testament and memorized by thousands.

The book begins with a simple, direct statement: "The word of the Lord . . . came to Joel" (Joel 1:1). The prophet's words are God's words, preserved for nearly three thousand years. No sooner is its message so described than Joel shocks his readers with the terse command, "Hear this!" (1:2). What follows is a divine selection of events and revelations about what will happen to the people of Israel and to the Gentile nations in the last days. Joel also contains a word from God for every age, startling in its simplicity and power.

The first chapter describes the effects of a plague of locusts which descended on Israel at some unknown time in the past. The second chapter compares the ancient plague to a predicted invasion by an army from the north in the latter days. The descriptions of the locusts and of the invaders are so intertwined that a few students think this chapter speaks only of an army of locusts, and not of an army of men as well. But portions of this chapter make such an explanation difficult to support. If Joel wrote only of the ancient plague of locusts, it is not easy to understand why there is no known record of a plague so dreadful that "there hath not been ever the like, neither shall be any more after it, even to the years of many generations" (Joel 2:2).

As the second chapter begins, the "day of the Lord" is near. Joel introduces the term "the day of the Lord" to Scripture. Other prophets develop it in both the Old and New Testaments, revealing that it will begin with the tribulation period and continue throughout the millennial kingdom of Christ. Daniel predicted "a time of trouble, such as never was since there was a nation" (Dan. 12:1), a statement much like Joel's. Christ quoted Daniel, and added the further revelation—similar to Joel's prophecy—that no such time of tribulation will ever occur again (Matt. 24:21).

As the day of the Lord dawns, a trumpet of alarm is sounded in Israel when a great host invades the land. It is called "the northern army" (Joel 2:20). The destructive power of the invaders is described in some detail: they turn the luxuriant countryside into a desolate wilderness. Fire and flame accompany them. There is a roar like that of heavy traffic or a blast furnace. The earth quakes, the heavens tremble, the sun and moon are darkened. A cry to God ascends from his ancient people. The Lord intervenes, destroys or drives the intruders away, restores rainfall and productivity to the land, pours out his Spirit, and blesses his people. The promise is made that they will never again know shame or reproach, for God will be in the midst of Israel from that time on.

The most satisfactory way to understand the second chapter of Joel is to recognize that an unmistakable picture emerges, against the background of a locust plague, of an army of men invading the land from the north, devastating it as the locusts did in the first chapter. Bible scholars are not in agreement as to how these two concepts can be reconciled in every verse of chapter 2. We do not have to solve this problem, nor do we have to be able to understand every verse clearly, in order to profit by this prophetic outline of future events. This is not the only place where Scripture moves from a description of present or past happenings to revelations about the distant future. For example, consider the famous prophecy in Isaiah of the virgin birth. A message to king Ahaz was made the basis for a divine announcement of the incarnation (Isa. 7:10-14).

Joel 2:1 speaks of the time when the day of the Lord will at last be near. The prophet paints a picture of what will be happening in Palestine as that day begins. The land will be called Israel (2:27). It will be populated by the children of Zion, i.e, the Jews (2:23). They will have returned to the land in unbelief. The absence of the blessing of God on them will be so evident that the nations will raise the question, "Where is their God?" (2:17). The Jews will have formed an independent nation, but will fear an invasion by other nations.

The land will have become like the garden of Eden under the hands of its ancient owners (Joel 2:2), in accordance with the divine principle that the mountains of Israel yield their fruit to the Jews (Ezek. 36:8). A temple will be standing in Jerusalem, attended by a Jewish priesthood (Joel 2:17). The climate will be dry; God will still be withholding the rain in his judgment on sin: "the Lord shall make the rain of thy land powder and dust" (Deut. 28:24). To the north of Israel a great and powerful military nation will threaten, causing greater fear than did Assyria or any other ancient aggressor (Joel 2:1, 2). This threat will culminate in an invasion.

The question is raised about whether the human race can survive: "The day of the Lord is great and very terrible; and who can abide it?" (Joel 2:11). Christ made a similar statement when he spoke of the coming great tribulation: "Except those days should be shortened, there should no flesh be saved: but for the elect's sake those days shall be shortened" (Matt. 24:22). Texts such as these have new meaning in our day when mankind faces the possibility of extinction through nuclear war.

From their despair the people of Israel will turn to the Lord for help. Trumpets will be sounded, the people will gather together, and a cry to God will be raised. Then the Lord will answer by removing the invaders, restoring rainfall to the land, and prospering his people, as he promised through Moses and the prophets. He will be present in person—"ye shall know that I am in the midst of Israel, and that I am the Lord your God" (Joel 2:27).

A careful comparison of Joel's prophecy about an invasion by a northern army and Ezekiel's description of an invasion from the north shows that the two are identical. Ezekiel prophesies the coming of a northern confederacy of nations against Israel, led by Gog, the prince of Rosh, generally understood to be the Soviet Union. Divine intervention destroys that army. Afterward, the Holy Spirit is poured out (Ezek. 39:29), as in Joel 2:28. Both prophets speak of Israel's knowing the Lord, who is in their midst after gathering them from the nations and causing his face to shine on them in blessing. The invasion evidently takes place during the tribulation period, before the Lord returns. However, it is not easy to determine precisely when it will occur within the chronology of the last days.

The last five verses of Joel 2 form a separate chapter in the Hebrew Bible. They stand out from the text as a sort of parenthesis. Peter quoted them on the day of Pentecost when he said, "This is that which was spoken by the prophet Joel" (Acts 2:16). It is important to notice that Peter did not say Joel's words were fulfilled at that time. Peter witnessed an outpouring of the Holy Spirit such as the prophet had predicted, but did not see the heavenly signs accompanying the future coming of the Spirit.

Joel predicted that all classes of people will prophesy and have dreams or see visions sent by God, without regard to age or condition. This is not what happened on the day the church was born, when a small company of Jewish disciples were filled with the Spirit and enabled to speak in the various languages of the nations represented in the assembled crowd.

Joel said the Spirit is to come "afterward." Peter used another expression. He said it would occur "in the last days," settling the question of where Joel's prophecy fits into the unfolding plan of God. Joel spoke primarily of the distant future, but a precursive fulfillment of his prophecy took place on the day of Pentecost. When the prophecy is actually fulfilled, the Spirit will be poured out on all flesh, after wonders have appeared in the heavens and in the earth. The sun will be turned into darkness and the moon into blood before the coming of the great and terrible day of the Lord.

One of the New Testament's best-known statements about the plan of salvation is taken from Joel 2:32: "Whosoever shall call on the name of the Lord shall be delivered." As quoted in Romans 10:13, it becomes, "Whosoever shall call upon the name of the Lord shall be saved." Calling on the name of the Lord brings salvation today, and it will bring deliverance for the people of Israel when the day of the Lord has come. The same truth was enunciated by David, "I will call upon the Lord, who is worthy to be praised: so shall I be saved from mine enemies" (Ps. 18:3).

The people of Israel and their land are the major emphases in Joel 2. The Gentile nations become an important theme in chapter 3. This chapter begins with time words clearly identifying the period in the divine program: "For, behold, in those days, and in that time, when I shall bring again the captivity of Judah and Jerusalem, I will also gather all nations" (Joel 3:1, 2). "Bringing again the captivity of the Jews" is a Hebrew idiom meaning God will restore their fortunes.

When the time has come for God to intervene in human history, he will gather all nations and bring them down into the valley of Jehoshaphat to sit in judgment over them. Other prophecies develop these events in great detail. The Lord spoke of them in Matthew 25:31, 32: "When the Son of man shall come in his glory, and all the holy angels with him, then shall he sit upon the throne of his glory: and before him shall be gathered all nations: and he shall separate them one from another, as a shepherd divideth his sheep from the goats."

The basis of this judgment is the way the Gentiles have treated the brethren of the Lord, called "my heritage Israel" in Joel 3:2. They have scattered the Jews among the nations, and anyone who touches the Jews touches the apple of the Lord's eye (Zech. 2:8). History is replete with examples of divine judgment on nations which mistreated Israel. Every nation will be present at the scene Joel describes. The Lord will bring them down into the valley of Jehoshaphat. The word translated "valley" emphasizes its depth. The common view that this refers to the depression between Jerusalem and the Mount of Olives (known as the valley of the Kidron) has no support in Scripture. The Bible never applies the name Jehoshaphat to the valley of the Kidron; the name has been popularly applied to it only since the fourth century.

The word "Jehoshaphat" means "Jehovah judges." It is the place where Jehovah will judge the nations. No one knows where this will be. Some have thought it may be Esdraelon. Others assume it will be the great valley created when the Lord returns (Zech. 14:4).

Joel informs us that, before the nations are judged, they will prepare for war and gather themselves together (at Armageddon, Rev. 16:16). God is behind this worldwide activity. He says, "I will gather all nations against Jerusalem to battle" (Zech. 14:2). Demons, always active in national affairs, will go forth to the kings of the earth "to gather them to the battle of that great day of God Almighty" (Rev. 16:14). Ploughshares and pruninghooks will be collected for use in the production of war material, in a great scrap drive like those of the two world wars.

The battle of Armageddon is to be no ordinary struggle of armed forces. It will be the culmination of the warfare which has cursed the earth for thousands of years, the last bloodbath before the inauguration of one thousand years of peace. These armies of the last days, under the leadership of the Antichrist, will actually attempt to make war against the Prince of glory as he returns to the earth accompanied by the armies of heaven (Rev. 19:14, 19). Joel speaks of this coming: "thither cause thy mighty ones to come down, O Lord" (Joel 3:11). The mighty ones include angels and glorified believers who once walked the earth: "The Lord my God shall come, and all the saints with thee" (Zech. 14:5); "When Christ, who is our life, shall appear, then shall ye also appear with him in glory" (Col. 3:4).

It will be the time when God harvests the earth. "Put ye in the sickle, for the harvest is ripe: come, get you down, for the press is full, the fats overflow; for their wickedness is great. Multitudes, multitudes in the valley of decision: for the day of the Lord is near in the valley of decision" (Joel 3:13, 14). In the parallel account in Revelation, "He that sat on the cloud thrust in his sickle on the earth; and the earth was reaped" (Rev. 14:16).

When God arises to shake the earth and to pour out his wrath, there will be convulsions of nature such as men have never seen. "The sun and the moon shall be darkened, and the stars shall withdraw their shining" (Joel 3:15). The heavens and the earth will shake as the Lord roars out of Zion and his voice is heard from Jerusalem. Earthquakes will change the face of the world and the greatest earthquake in history will take place (Rev. 16:18). The center of divine activity will be at Jerusalem. When the Lord returns, "his feet shall stand in that day upon the mount of Olives, which is before Jerusalem on the east, and the mount of Olives shall cleave in the midst thereof toward the east and toward the west" (Zech. 14:4).

Joel concludes his prophecy with a description of the glorious kingdom to be established after judgment has ended. The world will shine with millennial glory. The Lord will dwell in Zion, his high and holy mountain dominating the landscape of Israel. Jerusalem will be a holy city inhabited by the redeemed. The fertility of the land will be so great that it will again be known for its milk and honey. All the rivers will flow with water, ending more than two thousand years of barrenness. A spring will flow from the house of the Lord, rising from a subterranean source. A great river will refresh the lower Jordan valley, changing the sterile waters of the Dead Sea into a freshwater lake containing "a very great multitude of fish" (Ezek. 47:9; see 47:1-12).

The words "Judah shall dwell forever" do not mean the

present earth will be the dwelling place of Israel for eternity. There is no word in Hebrew carrying the meaning of our word "eternity." The root translated "forever" means literally, "unto ends of days," or "until time out of mind." The state of affairs described by Joel will continue throughout the kingdom age, until God's purposes for his land and his earthly people have been accomplished. Until that time, the people of Israel will dwell in their ancient land, its curse removed, in the center of a peaceful world.

The Bible carries the future of the Jews on into eternity. For example, here's what Jeremiah wrote about the natural laws which God established to govern the heavenly bodies: "If those ordinances depart from before me, saith the Lord, then the seed of Israel also shall cease from being a nation before me for ever" (Jer. 31:36). The present heaven and earth will pass away, but God's chosen people will continue to live in his presence (Isa. 65:17).

Joel's prophecy is among the most important and practical revelations in the Bible. What is the responsibility of the people of God when the day of the Lord is near at hand? It is the same as it has been in every time of trouble, when human resources have come to an end and men's hearts have failed them for fear of what lies ahead. Joel's answer comes immediately after the question is raised, "The day of the Lord is great and very terrible; and who can abide it?" (Joel 2:11). Israel's responsibility and ours is found in the words, "Therefore also now, saith the Lord, Turn ye even to me with all your heart, and with fasting, and with weeping, and with mourning" (2:12).

Omitting the word "even," which is not in the original text, there are eight monosyllables in this exhortation: "Turn ye . . . to me with all your heart." It is much like other admonitions calling for wholehearted obedience to God. When we need to know his will, it is, "Trust in the Lord with all thine heart" (Prov. 3:5). In times of declension, it is, "Serve the Lord thy God with all your heart" (1 Sam. 12:20). In days when his blessing is in evidence, we are told, "Love the Lord thy God with all thine heart" (Deut. 30:6).

After the Jewish people have returned in large numbers to their land in unbelief, and are surrounded and attacked by vastly superior forces, with no possible escape, there will be only one answer to their terrible predicament. They must turn to the Lord, the God of their fathers, with all their hearts. When they do, he will deliver them.

The details of what such a turning to the Lord means may sound strange to us today. There will be fasting, weeping, and mourning. An affluent generation long free from affliction knows nothing of such words. But here they are, God's counsel for people faced with imminent calamity. The study of prophecy brings many blessings, but it also brings to light some solemn warnings. The day of the Lord will eventually mean wonderful things for the human race, but it is to begin with great troubles. "Woe unto you that desire the day of the Lord! to what end is it for you? the day of the Lord is darkness, and not light" (Amos 5:18).

The ministers of the Lord are instructed to weep between the porch and the altar (Joel 2:17). The porch was the vestibule of the ancient temple from which God's message was given. The altar was the place where God provided a sacrifice for sin and where he spoke to his servants. The priests of Israel, then, deeply moved by the pending tragedy and their own dreadful responsibility, are enjoined to weep before they give God's message to the people. Any ambassador of Christ knows that tears often accompany the divine call.

Yet, "he that goeth forth and weepeth, bearing precious seed, shall doubtless come again with rejoicing, bringing his sheaves with him" (Ps. 126:6). The apostle Paul knew this. He reminded the people of Ephesus, "Remember, that by the space of three years I ceased not to warn every one night and day with tears" (Acts 20:31).

In a message on Joel 2:12, Alexander Whyte of Edinburgh commented on this theme:

As you come down the Old and the New Testaments you will be astonished and encouraged to find how prevailing a fountain of tears always is with God . . . David with his swimming bed; Jeremiah with his head waters; Mary Magdalene over his feet with her welling eyes; Peter's bitter cry all his life long, as often as he heard a cock crow, and so on. So on through a multitude whose names are written in heaven, and who went up to heaven all the way with inconsolable sorrow because of their sins. They took words and turned to the Lord; but, better than the best words, they took tears, or rather, their tears took them. The best words, the words that the Holy Spirit himself teacheth, if they are without tears, will avail nothing. Even inspired words will not pass through, while all the time tears, mere tears, without words, are omnipotent with God. Words weary him, while tears overcome and command him. He inhabits the tears of Israel. . . . It is the same with ourselves. Tears move us, tears melt us, we cannot resist tears.

The nations will say about Israel, "Where is their God?" There surely ought to be some evidence of the supernatural among Christians today. If there is none, the world cannot be blamed for wondering where our God is. Elisha expected visible evidence of God's presence when he cried, "Where is the Lord God of Elijah?" (2 Kings 2:14). God answered him with fire from heaven. The great evangelist Finney was deeply moved by the fact the prayers in his church were not answered, and that no one seemed to expect them to be answered. He went out into the forest and wrestled with God until he received assurance that the Lord would manifest himself through Finney. Many of God's people have had prayer answered in such an unmistakable way. When the ministers of Israel confidently expect divine intervention as their land is invaded in the last days, they will receive an answer to God's promise: "Call unto me, and I will answer thee, and shew thee great and mighty things, which thou knowest not" (Jer. 33:3).

In Joel's prophecy, God's response will be immediate: "Then will the Lord be jealous for his land, and pity his people, Yea, the Lord will answer" (Joel 2:18, 19). The entire book is built around this divine certainty. The terrible locust plague, the invasion by armies from the north, the turning of Israel to the Lord, the blessings which follow, the judgment of the nations, and the coming of the kingdom are clustered around this revelation. Everything will happen just as it is written.

CHAPTER 6
CHRIST'S
GREATEST PROPHECY

The major prophecy of the New Testament, apart from the Book of Revelation, is the Olivet Discourse, recorded in its most complete form in Matthew 24 and 25. It forms a bridge between the Old Testament prophets and the Revelation. Few books have been written about it, even though it is longer than the Sermon on the Mount, about which there has been considerable writing. Many regard the Discourse as mysterious and hard to understand. Called by some "an obscure apocalyptic," it is actually one of the clearest prophecies to be found anywhere in the Bible, remarkably free from figures of speech. Taken literally, it is an orderly and progressive outline of coming events, written in the plainest language.

The Olivet Discourse contains the New Testament's greatest concentration of references to the end times. There are fifteen specific mentions of the end, or of Christ's coming, in these two chapters. More time words and definite signs are given than anywhere else within such a brief compass. This fact alone makes it evident that Christ was not speaking of the present age—no signs were given to mark the conclusion of the present age. Moreover, the church was still an unrevealed part of the divine program when Christ spoke these words (Matt. 16:18).

Israel is clearly the primary theme. Christ's lament over the city of Jerusalem sets the stage for the Discourse. In reference to the Jewish temple, he said, "There shall not be left here one stone upon another, that shall not be thrown down" (Matt. 24:1, 2). His words gave rise to the disciples' questions and called forth the Discourse.

Throughout Matthew 24 we find statements that refer to

the Jewish people alone. It is the residents of Judaea who are warned to flee a coming time of tribulation (24:16). The sign by which they will know when to leave their land is the "abomination of desolation" (24:15), standing in the holy place of the Jerusalem temple. Daniel placed this event in the middle of the final seven years of Israel's troubled history, prior to the return of Christ (Dan. 9:27). The tribulation awaiting Israel in the last days is the theme of many prophecies, beginning with Moses' words uttered thirty-five hundred years ago: "When thou art in tribulation . . . even in the latter days" (Deut. 4:30).

Those who flee are told to "pray [that their] flight be not in the winter, neither on the sabbath day" (Matt. 24:20), a strange prayer indeed for Christians, and not found on any believer's prayer list. The warning against false Christs (24:24) is intended for Jewish people awaiting their Messiah. Christians having already found him could not easily be deceived by a counterfeit. The shortening of the days in 24:22 is an Old Testament theme relating to Israel (Amos 8:9). Signs involving the sun, moon, and stars are given to Israel and Jerusalem, but never to the church (Matt. 24:29; Joel 3:15, 16).

The mourning tribes of Matthew 24:30 are the tribes of Israel (Zech. 12:10-14). The word for tribes is used of Israel in six other places in the New Testament, but never of the Gentiles or the church (James 1:1). The sign of the fig tree is generally understood to be a reference to the Jews (Matt. 24:32). The judgment scene of Matthew 25:31-46 is also described in the prophecy of Joel 3:1, 2. Its basis is the way the nations, or Gentiles, have treated the Jews, Christ's brethren according to the flesh.

Statements like these are woven into the fabric of the Olivet Discourse. The prophecy is a self-contained unit. To interrupt it at any place with speculative interpretations about the present age is to destroy this unity. God has given us sufficient truth about the present age. We must not take from the people of Israel a part of the Bible given specifically for their instruction and admonition.

It is remarkable to note the progress of thought in Christ's great prophecy. Important time words divide it into orderly and progressive parts. There is to be a beginning of sorrows which leads to a definite end. A time of great tribulation is to be followed by the coming of the Son of man in glory. After he comes, he will sit on the throne of his glory judging the nations. Then his kingdom will be established. The order of events cannot be changed.

The first division of the Discourse speaks of war, famine, pestilence, and earthquake, called "the beginning of sorrows" (Matt. 24:8). The word translated "sorrows" is literally "birth pangs." It is taken from the Old Testament description of the anguish of Israel during the tribulation. The Talmud and the Midrash frequently speak of the birth pangs of the Messiah. The expression is found in Jewish Orthodox doctrine today. The Bible calls these pangs the great tribulation, a period of pain and suffering which precedes deliverance and a kingdom characterized by happiness and blessing. Isaiah asks, "Shall a nation be born at once? for as soon as Zion travailed, she brought forth her children" (Isa. 66:8). The expression appears in the New Testament with reference to the same period: "When they shall say, Peace and safety; then sudden destruction cometh upon them, as travail upon a woman with child; and they shall not escape" (1 Thess. 5:3).

Some have assumed that the beginning verses of Matthew 24 describe the present age. They argue that war and other evils have been frequently occurring since apostolic times; however, this was also true of previous ages. If Christ were speaking of the present age, it would be an anachronism for him to describe a period not yet known to prophecy, about which his followers were still in darkness. There is a remarkable parallel between these verses and the opening of the seals in Revelation 6—these introduce the tribulation as the time when such great evils will come upon mankind.

Revelation places a concentration of war, famine, pestilence, martyrdom, and earthquake early in the time of Jacob's trouble. What Christ said is in perfect agreement with this. If this portion of Matthew 24 speaks of the age of the church, we are faced with the anomaly of birth pangs continuing for more than nineteen hundred years. Such pangs belong properly to the brief time in the future of which Jeremiah wrote, "Wherefore do I see every man with his hands on his loins, as a woman in travail, and all faces turned into paleness? Alas! for that day is great, so that none is like it: it is even the time of Jacob's trouble, but he shall be saved out of it" (Jer. 30:6, 7).

Another time word appears in Matthew 24:9: "*Then* shall they deliver you up to be afflicted, and shall kill you: and ye shall be hated of all nations for my name's sake." In this passage, the "you" is not the church. The church will not even be present on the earth during the tribulation. Rather, the "you" refers to the Jews who will be living during the time of what Jeremiah called "Jacob's trouble."

It is a serious mistake to assume that the words, "he that shall endure unto the end, the same shall be saved" (Matt. 24:13) relate to the divine plan of salvation. No passage of Scripture teaches that men are saved eternally on the basis of their endurance. Our Lord was actually speaking of the salvation ·or deliverance of "tribulation saints" who are still living at the end of that time of distress. They will be saved by the second coming of our Lord, and will enter the kingdom.

One of the most misunderstood verses in the Olivet Discourse is the statement: "This gospel of the kingdom shall be preached in all the world for a witness unto all nations; and then shall the end come" (Matt. 24:14). The gospel of the kingdom must be distinguished from the good news of the grace of God (Acts 20:24), called "the gospel of Christ" a dozen times in the epistles (2 Cor. 4:3-6). The gospel of Christ is defined as the good news of Christ's death, burial, and resurrection on our behalf (1 Cor. 15:1-4). The gospel of the kingdom is the message that Christ and the disciples proclaimed when the kingdom was being offered to the people of Israel: "Repent: for the kingdom of heaven is at hand" (Matt. 4:17; see also 4:23; 10:7). No evangelist or missionary in the present age would preach this message, for the kingdom is not now being offered as it was during Christ's earthly ministry. The gospel of Christ is, "Believe on the Lord Jesus Christ, and thou shalt be saved" (Acts 16:31). When the tribulation arrives, the good news of the nearness of the kingdom will once more be proclaimed. Then Israel will repent, and the kingdom will be established in the earth.

During the tribulation, Jewish people will be divinely chosen to announce this good news: "An hundred and forty and four thousand of all the tribes of the children of Israel" (Rev. 7:4) are set apart as servants of God at that time (see 7:1-8). Their mission will be successful. We read of "a great multitude, which no man could number, of all nations, and kindreds, and people, and tongues" (7:9) who come out of the great tribulation, cleansed by the blood of the Lamb (7:9-14). Today, missionaries must learn the languages of the people to whom they are sent. When the church is gone, God's chosen messengers will be from among the twelve tribes. They will providentially be prepared for their task, for they will know the languages of the nations among whom they are scattered. They will preach "in all the world for a witness unto all nations" (Matt. 24:14). The end will come after their work is done, and the nations will be judged for the way they have treated these brethren of Christ (25:40).

One of the most important signs anywhere in prophetic literature is "the abomination of desolation, . . . [standing] in the holy place" (Matt. 24:15). When Christ warned of this he was quoting Daniel, who spoke of it three times (e.g., Dan. 9:27). In Old Testament times, an abomination was an image to which worship was offered, such as Ashtoreth, the abomination of the Zidonians (2 Kings 23:13). The false prophet of the last days will make such an image during the time of Jacob's trouble. He will require that everyone worship it (Rev. 13:14, 15).

The image will stand in the holy place. There was a holy place in the tabernacle of the wilderness (Exod. 28:29), in the temple of Solomon (2 Chron. 4:22), and in the temple of Herod (Acts 21:28). There will also be a holy place in the millennial temple (Ezek. 42:14). The abomination of which Christ spoke will stand in the holy place of the tribulation temple (Rev. 11:1, 2; 2 Thess. 2:4). When the Jews of that day who believe the words of Christ see the abomination standing there, they will flee into the mountains. They will find refuge in the wilderness (Rev. 12:14). It has been suggested that this "wilderness" may be Petra, a remote and inaccessible valley in the land of Moab, where an ancient city was carved out of the rocky cliffs.

The placing of the abomination in the holy place marks the beginning of a terrible crisis for the Jewish people. They are warned to flee Judaea immediately, leaving everything behind. In view of what the Lord said about flight on the Sabbath (Matt. 24:20), it is remarkable that in Israel today, transportation is practically shut down on the Sabbath, and the food stores are all closed.

The absence of any such warning to the church to flee the terrors of the tribulation is a convincing indication that the church will not be present on the earth in those days. Christ will have fulfilled the following promise before these things take place: "I also will keep thee from the hour of temptation, which shall come upon all the world, to try them that dwell upon the earth" (Rev. 3:10).

Not everyone agrees about the precise meaning of this prophecy uttered by Christ: "Except those days should be shortened, there should no flesh be saved: but for the elect's sake those days shall be shortened" (Matt. 24:22). Some have suggested that the period of tribulation will be shortened, making it less than seven years long, but this would invalidate Daniel's specific prophecy, and the parallel passages in Revelation 11:2, 3; 12:6; 13:5.

A more satisfactory explanation is that the passage means just what it says—the days themselves will be made short. Amos predicted that the sun will go down at noon on that day (Amos 8:9). Revelation speaks of the smiting of the sun, moon, and stars, reducing the daylight hours by one-third (Rev. 8:12). Such texts call for days shorter than the normal twenty-four hours, preceded by heavenly disturbances and violent changes on earth.

Whatever form this shortening of the days may take, it will be for the sake of the elect. In Old Testament days the Jewish people were God's elect (Isa. 45:4). During the present age believers who form the true church are called "God's elect" (see Rom. 8:28-33). After the church has been translated to heaven, all who have believed God's message for that time will constitute the elect. The "elect" appears again in Matthew 24:24. False Christs and false prophets will show signs and wonders great enough to deceive the very elect, if that were possible. It is sobering to learn that miracles in the last days are to characterize false prophets rather than true men of God.

Beginning with Matthew 24:27, the second coming of Christ is described at length. Christ will not be found in some desert place, nor will he come as a mystic holding forth in a curtained retreat. He will come in a manner as instantaneous and as shocking as a flash of lightning.

Christ's first words after speaking of the coming of the Son of man have puzzled many: "For wheresoever the carcase is, there will the eagles be gathered together" (Matt. 24:28). There are many ideas about what these words mean. A respected commentary declares that the carcass is "the spiritually dead and decaying mass of the wicked," while the eagles or vultures are "the agents of divine judgment." Some have imagined that the carcass represents Israel or Jerusalem. One of the strangest theories says that the carcass is Christ's body, to which Christians "flock like vultures."

There is no good reason to suppose that the Lord was concealing truth under obscure figures of speech. Elsewhere it is revealed that when he comes and destroys the armies of the Antichrist, the fowls of the air will gather together "unto the supper of the great God" (Rev. 19:17). This extended prophecy is in perfect agreement with Christ's brief mention of this great event in connection with his return. His words might not be written off as too abstract if it were remembered that a key to this reference to vultures or eagles is found in Job 39:30: "Where the slain are, there is she."

Some of the time words which abound in the Discourse appear in Matthew 24:29, 30: "*Immediately after* the tribulation of those days shall the sun be darkened, and the moon shall not give her light, and the stars shall fall from heaven, and the powers of the heavens shall be shaken: and *then* shall appear the sign of the Son of man in heaven: and *then* shall all the tribes of the earth mourn, and they shall see the Son of man coming in the clouds of heaven with power and great glory" (italics mine).

We do not know the meaning of the sign of the Son of man. It has been suggested it may be the Shekinah glory, or the cross, or simply the Lord himself. The tribes who mourn are the people of Israel—the word for "tribes" is used only of Israel in the New Testament. They see the One whom they pierced, recognize him as their true Messiah, and mourn for him, as Zechariah predicted (Zech. 12:10). "Every eye shall see him, and they also which pierced him: and all kindreds of the earth shall wail because of him" (Rev. 1:7). This mourning is contrasted with the joy of the church at the rapture (1 Pet. 4:13).

After the Lord has returned, he will "send his angels with a great sound of a trumpet, and they shall gather together his elect from the four winds, from one end of heaven to the other" (Matt. 24:31). This fulfills the promise given to Moses that the Lord "will return and gather thee from all the nations, wither the Lord thy God hath scattered thee" (Deut. 30:3). It represents a use of Old Testament language referring to Israel. The sound of the trumpet brought the Jews together in ancient times (Num. 10:7). The Jews have been scattered abroad "as the four winds of the heaven" (Zech. 2:6). Moses spoke of their being driven out to the outmost parts of heaven (Deut. 30:4). Isaiah prophesied that the people of Israel

—God's elect—would inherit and dwell in the promised land (Isa. 65:9).

At this point in the Discourse, the Lord has returned and gathered his earthly people together. His mode of address changes. He speaks of the time of his coming, and the scenes of judgment it will bring to the people of Israel. Christ's parable of the fig tree is recognized as a reference to the Jews (Joel 1:7). Just as the budding of the fig tree in nature indicates summer is near, so the coming of the things Christ speaks about will indicate the nearness of the end. "This generation shall not pass, till all these things be fulfilled" (Matt. 24:34). The simplest explanation of this verse is the true one. The generation that sees the coming of the tribulation, with all its signs, will see the consummation. Another widely accepted view of this passage is that the word "generation" means the race or family of Israel, which will continue to exist until all things are fulfilled.

The folly of attempting to set dates on the basis of what is revealed here is evident from the declaration: no one but the Father knows when that day and hour will come (24:36).

This central section of the Discourse shows great diversity. There are seven illustrations: the fig tree, the flood of Noah, the two workers, the householder, the two servants, the ten virgins, and the talents. Three prophetic themes are emphasized: (1) The Lord's return will find unawareness amounting to blindness with regard to coming judgment; (2) there will be a separation of men into two classes, with rewards for the righteous and punishment for the wicked; and (3) it is necessary for men to be watchful in view of the return of the Son of man.

The illustration of the Great Flood sets the stage for what follows. The wicked were unaware of what was coming until they were all taken away by the waters. Noah was left to enjoy the blessings of God on a cleansed earth. This was a divine act involving the entire human race, implying universal judgment to come. It went beyond the people of Israel to all humankind. The Discourse makes it perfectly clear that the coming of the Son of man will be like the days of Noah—some will be taken away in judgment at his return, just as men were taken away in judgment by the flood.

In Noah's day those who were left behind were blessed on the cleansed earth. When Christ comes in judgment, those left behind will be blessed in the ensuing kingdom. The same truth is taught in the Lord's explanation of the parable of the tares: the wicked are gathered together and cast into a furnace of fire, while the righteous enter the kingdom (Matt. 13:41-43). The word used for "taking away" in Matthew 24:40, 41, while sometimes used in a good sense (20:17), is used of the Lord's being taken away to be crucified (John 19:16) and of Paul's being taken away to prison (Acts 23:18).

"One shall be taken, and the other left" (Matt. 24:40). This verse is sometimes quoted in connection with the rapture of the church. But it is incorrect to do so. In this verse Matthew is describing a scene of judgment. The church cannot be introduced here without violating the entire context. In the same chapter the evil servant is taken away to a place of weeping and gnashing of teeth (Matt. 24:51). The wicked servant is cast into outer darkness (25:26-30). The foolish virgins are shut out from the presence of the bridegroom (25:10). In the final judgment scene the cursed are cast into everlasting fire (25:31-46). All of these passages have to do with what happens at the return of the Son of man to the earth. They do not refer to the rapture, even though it is true that at that time some will be taken away (for blessing) while some will be left behind (for judgment).

The content of this portion of the Olivet Discourse is so rich that it is often used to illustrate eternal principles. The illustration of the householder teaches the need for watchfulness—no one knows when the Son of man will come (Matt. 24:43, 44). The two servants represent the impossibility of knowing when the Lord will return; they also illustrate the rewarding of some and the casting out of others in that day (24:45-51). The ten virgins, who represent the people of Israel on earth at his coming, illustrate the unexpectedness of his return, the need for watchfulness, and the rewarding of the wise and the closing of the door on the foolish (25:1-13). The story of the talents teaches the eternal principle that faithfulness, rather than personal ability or opportunity, is the basis for rewards (25:14-30).

The Olivet Discourse begins with an extended section devoted primarily to the people of Israel; it concludes with a section given primarily to the subject of the Gentile nations. At the end of the Discourse, the Lord is still speaking of the time "when the Son of man shall come in his glory" (Matt. 25:31). This is not to be confused with the judgment of the great white throne, when the wicked dead are judged long after Christ has returned to the earth. When the Lord fulfills his promise by returning to the earth in power and glory (24:30), he will sit on the throne of his glory and gather all nations before him.

The word translated "nations" (Matt. 25:32) may also be rendered "Gentiles." We need not assume these nations are political states; judgment shall be individual. It is possible that these are the Gentiles whom the Lord brought together for Armageddon (Zech. 14:2), because a similar time of judgment is described in Matthew 24:40, 41.

The Gentiles, or nations, are judged on the basis of the way they have treated the "brethren of Christ." Joel identified these brethren as Jews, when he describes the judgment of the nations in the valley of Jehoshaphat on the basis of the way they treated "my people and . . . my heritage Israel" (Joel 3:2).

The two most prominent words found in the prediction of Genesis 12:3 reappear here. God said to Abraham: "I will bless them that bless thee and curse him that curseth thee." The final fulfillment of this word is seen as the Lord returns. He says to the righteous, "Come, ye blessed of my Father, inherit the kingdom prepared for you from the foundation of the world" (Matt. 25:34). To the wicked he says, "Depart from me, ye cursed, into everlasting fire" (24:41; cf. Ps. 37:22).

The concluding verses of Matthew 25 carry these two companies all the way into eternity. The righteous people of the kingdom go on to enjoy life eternal, while the wicked experience everlasting punishment.

PART II
THE FUTURE
OF THE GENTILES

CHAPTER 7
THE UNITED STATES
AND OTHER NATIONS

The Bible mentions the peoples of the world approximately 760 times. This fact is obscured by the use of four different English words to translate the Old Testament (Hebrew) word *goy* and the equivalent New Testament (Greek) word *ethnos*. The four words are "nations," "Gentiles," "heathen," and "people." They usually occur in the plural. *Goy* appears 600 times, *ethnos* is found 160 times.

When such words are found in our Bibles, they do not necessarily refer to political states or countries. They often mean simply Gentiles as opposed to Jews, as in Acts 11:1: "the Gentiles . . . also received the word of God." When we read that all nations will be gathered before the Lord at his return (Matt. 25:32), it may be easier to understand this prophecy if we think of individual Gentiles rather than Gentile nations.

Prior to the present century the subject of the nations in prophecy was seldom discussed. No messages on this theme appear in anthologies of sermons delivered at prophetic conferences in the late nineteenth century. Bible dictionaries and encyclopedias offer little information about it. A survey of prophecy published as recently as 1958 contains a bibliography of nearly three hundred books and articles covering the whole field of Bible prophecy. It lists no books about the nations; only one short magazine article is cited.

We are now living in the extended period of history called "the times of the Gentiles" (Luke 21:24). They have ruled the world for twenty-five hundred years, ever since God took away sovereignty from the people of Israel and gave it to Nebuchadnezzar, who was told, "Wheresoever the children of men dwell . . . hath he given into thine hand, and hath made thee ruler over them all" (Dan. 2:38). Cyrus, king of Persia, was able to say, "The Lord God of heaven hath given me all the kingdoms of the earth" (Ezra 1:2). Until the day comes when God restores Israel to divine favor and makes her the leading nation of the world, he will continue to deal with all nations on the basis of clearly stated principles, at least five of which are revealed in Scripture.

The first principle is that God will prosper any nation which seeks to please him: "Blessed is the nation whose God is the Lord" (Ps. 33:12); "The wicked shall be turned into hell, and all the nations that forget God" (Ps. 9:17); "The nation and kingdom that will not serve thee shall perish; yea, those nations shall be utterly wasted" (Isa. 60:12). Illustrations of the truth of this principle abound in the Bible. The Philistines were destroyed (Zeph. 2:5), Edom was desolated, and Elam was consumed (Jer. 49:17, 37). The Roman Empire perished because of its godlessness. Parallels have been drawn between the decline and fall of the Empire and its failure to honor the Word of God. On the other hand, the United States is often cited as an example of a nation favored by God because it has historically acknowledged him.

A second principle has to do with the law of God. "Righteousness exalteth a nation: but sin is a reproach to any people" (Prov. 14:34). God's laws are best exemplified in the Ten Commandments. Nations fall when they disobey God's holy law. An example of this principle is seen in the story of the Amorites who once inhabited Palestine. God said to Abram on one occasion, "The iniquity of the Amorites is not yet full" (Gen. 15:16). When the wickedness of this people later reached the point where God would permit it no longer, he destroyed them (Acts 13:19). Fire fell from heaven on Sodom and Gomorrah because of their great sin (Gen. 19:13). When Nineveh repented of its sin under the preaching of Jonah, its judgment was postponed (Jon. 1:2; 3:10). Pompeii doubtlessly belongs in a list of such wicked people. "Behold, the eyes of the Lord are upon the sinful kingdom, and I will destroy it from off the face of the earth" (Amos 9:8).

A third—perhaps the best known—principle determining the fate of nations was given by God to Abram, progenitor of the Hebrews: "I will bless them that bless thee, and curse him that curseth thee" (Gen. 12:3). Throughout history the blessing of God has indeed rested on nations and individuals who have been good to the Jewish people. His judgment has come on those who have not. Assyria, Babylon, and Nazi Germany are outstanding examples. The beginning of the decline of Spain can be traced back to its expulsion of all Jews in 1492.

A fourth principle is related to God's purpose to save individuals from eternal death. The Lord is "not willing that any should perish, but that all should come to repentance. . . . [T]he longsuffering of our Lord is salvation" (2 Pet. 3:9, 15). One reason he allows evil to continue and wicked nations to remain unpunished for a time is that he is now taking out from among the Gentiles a people for his name (Acts 15:14). This purpose takes precedence over the punishment of evildoers, whose time will come later. Christ told his disciples, "Repentance and remission of sins should be preached in [my] name among all nations" (Luke 24:47). Where the work of the gospel is encouraged, divine favor is likely to be manifested. Where it is opposed and hindered by the government, national destruction is sure to come.

Any consideration of Bible statements about the fate of nations should include what may be regarded as a fifth principle: satanic influence weakens the nations (Isa. 14:12). The devil "deceiveth the whole world" (Rev. 12:9), and he deceives the nations and leads them into wars which destroy them (20:8). The ancient nations of Greece and Persia were influenced or controlled by the evil forces of the unseen world (Dan. 10:13, 20). Demonic powers are also at work in modern political states, seeking to frustrate the purposes of God and to further the kingdom of Satan. Some actions of world powers can be understood only in the light of these divine revelations. When national leaders become involved in astrology and the occult, giving heed to seducing spirits and messages from the forbidden unseen world, there is danger of national decay and ruin.

Jerusalem occupies an important place in the events leading to the final end of Gentile times. Christ said, "Jerusalem shall be trodden down of the Gentiles, until the times of the Gentiles be fulfilled" (Luke 21:24). An examination of the way in which the Lord used the expression "until the times be fulfilled" elsewhere (Mark 1:15) can lead to the conclusion that when the city of Jerusalem fell to Jewish armies in 1967—for the first time in twenty-five hundred years—an important milestone in the times of the Gentiles was reached (Mark 1:14, 15). The end of those times could be approaching quickly.

The only nations mentioned in Old Testament history were those which had direct contact with Israel. The same thing is true about prophecy dealing with the latter days. The question of why today's great nations are not named in Scripture is answered by the fact that the Bible deals primarily with events involving Israel. Some nations existing in the last times are named, but most are not. Nevertheless, there are at least sixty clear statements about *all* nations. It is this body of prophetic truth which must be examined for light on what is going to happen to America and other nations during the closing years of world history.

Many attempts have been made to find America in the prophetic Scriptures. All of them have been rejected by conservative students as violating sound rules of exegesis.

The best known of these efforts is based on a few words in Ezekiel 38:13, where "the merchants of Tarshish, with all the young lions thereof" protest against the invasion of the land of Israel by a northern confederacy of nations. It was suggested that Tarshish is to be identified as England, and that America is one of the young lions, or "colonies," of England. The ridiculous notion has been put forth that because the United States has a large aircraft industry, it is Isaiah's "land shadowing with wings" (Isa. 18:1). More recently attempts have been made to draw parallels between America and Babylon. Another theory is that the United States will become an unimportant second-rate power after the rapture, since the sudden removal of large numbers of believers from places of leadership in government and industry will produce chaos so great the nation will be unable to recover. Meanwhile, atheistic Russia will not be affected.

Whatever value some find in these ideas about the future, any such speculation tends to obscure the fact that a considerable amount of prophecy has been given about all nations in the last days. If the United States or any other nation exists at that time, everything written about all nations naturally applies to the United States or any other such nation. There is no reason why individual countries should be named in Scripture. There can be no doubt that America has as good a chance as any nation of being in existence in the closing days of history. No other nation has gone beyond America in honoring the principles of Scripture. Few have equalled it. The Ten Commandments underlie our laws. We have befriended the Jewish people. Our land has been a missionary stronghold. Despite our tragic failures, there is reason to hope America will not perish from the earth.

Revelation about all nations in the last days is made up of two kinds of passages: those which mention all nations, and those which speak of events and conditions involving the whole world. By examining such prophecies, we can determine something of what will happen to the people and land of the United States during the last days:

1. America will lose all its Christians. The people of God are awaiting the rapture. This translation of all Christians from earth to heaven is the next event prophesied in the Bible (1 Thess. 4:13-18). When it takes place, and every true believer is gone forever, the consequences for our society can hardly be imagined. The nation will be deprived of countless leaders in government, industry, education, social service, agriculture,

and medicine. Christian organizations will no longer exist. The vast sums now contributed by believers to charitable works of every kind will no longer be available. No one can evaluate the importance of prayers, intercession, and thanksgivings now being offered up by Christians on behalf of all who are in authority (see 1 Tim. 2:1, 2). It seems inevitable that the sudden removal of a considerable part of the population will strike terror into the hearts of great numbers of people who are left behind.

2. Lawlessness and evil will exceed anything ever known in history. The Bible declares that the present divine restraint on lawlessness or iniquity will someday come to an end: "He who now restrains will continue to restrain, until he be taken out of the way" (2 Thess. 2:7, lit.). The language of the text in the original makes it clear this restrainer is an individual. He is not named, but it is believed he is the Holy Spirit, now resident in the church (1 Cor. 3:16). Christ promised the Spirit would abide with his followers forever (John 14:16). The world has never been able to receive him; he came to dwell on the·earth only after there was a people here prepared to receive him (John 14:17). When the church is removed from the earth, the Holy Spirit's temple will be gone, and with it the restraining presence of the Spirit of God, which has blessed the world since the day of Pentecost.

Sir Robert Anderson, an evangelical Christian, was head of Scotland Yard early in the twentieth century. One evening on a London street a friend asked him, "You say the London police are outnumbered by the people of the underworld. Why does the underworld not take over the city?" Sir Robert pointed to a gospel service being conducted nearby and replied, "There is the reason. The Holy Spirit indwells all Christians and holds back the tide of evil. Some day God will take his church away. Then restraint will be gone, and I believe the underworld will indeed take over the city." The time after the rapture will be like the days of Noah, when violence filled the earth, and like the days of Lot, when perversion brought judgment on Sodom and Gomorrah (Luke 17:26-28).

3. Our nation will experience the worst time of distress and affliction it has ever known, as God punishes the inhabitants of the earth for their iniquity (Isa. 26:21). This "time of trouble, such as never was since there was a nation even to that same time" (Dan. 12:1) will involve every nation under heaven: "The indignation of the Lord will come upon all nations, and his fury upon all their armies" (Isa. 34:2). In the words of Christ, there will be "distress of nations, with perplexity" (Luke 21:25). Citizens of every country will fear "those things which are coming on the earth" (21:26). When that dreadful time is over, nothing like it will ever be seen again (Matt. 24:21). Scripture is so explicit about the coming tribulation that the subject is usually treated separately in studies of prophecy.

4. During America's unparalleled time of trouble, a great many people will turn to the Lord in a remarkable spiritual awakening. In Revelation 7 we read that this awakening will occur immediately after God chooses 144,000 servants from among the twelve tribes of Israel as his representatives, in the absence of the raptured missionaries of the cross. The Jewish people at that time will still be scattered among all nations, and God's chosen company will undoubtedly be familiar with most of the world's languages. After God has called and set them apart for their work, "a great multitude, which no man could number, of all nations, and kindreds, and people, and tongues" (7:9) will come out of the great tribulation, having been cleansed by the blood of the Lamb.

5. America will come under the rule of the Antichrist during this same period. No nation can be excluded from what is written about this evil being: "Power was given him over all kindreds, and tongues, and nations" (Rev. 13:7). We have no details as to how the beast will rule, but this passage points to the end of democracy as the United States has known it. The Antichrist will become the object of international worship, and he will control the world economy. People will not be able to do business in America or anywhere else unless they bear the mark of the beast on their right hands or on their foreheads (13:8, 16, 17).

6. Near the end of the tribulation, American troops will invade Palestine under the banner of the Antichrist. The Lord has said, "I will gather all nations against Jerusalem to battle" (Zech. 14:2). Demonic powers will gather "the kings of the earth and of the whole world . . . to the battle of that great day of God Almighty" (Rev. 16:14). The climax of the battle will be reached when the Antichrist, drunk with power, thinks he can prevail against the returning Lord and the armies of heaven: "And I saw the beast, and the kings of the earth, and their armies, gathered together to make war against him that sat on the horse, and against his army" (19:19). Inevitably, the Antichrist and his forces will be soundly defeated.

7. The United States must someday lose all its Jews. God has promised Israel, "I will take you from among the heathen, and gather you out of all countries, and will bring you into your own land" (Ezek. 36:24). Scores of similar passages are scattered throughout the Bible. No part of the Jewish population will remain behind. Ezekiel declares the Lord will leave none of them where they have been scattered (39:28). The effect of this on America can hardly be imagined. Jewish people occupy places of leadership in every walk of life, far out of proportion to their population. Their God-given "power to get wealth" is legendary (Deut. 8:18). The wisdom and skill they have brought to medicine, industry, business, science, and other fields will all be transferred to the land of Israel. Every nation will lose some of its most brilliant leaders.

8. When Christ returns he will sit on the throne of his glory judging the nations (Matt. 25:31, 32). It is impossible to exclude America from this well-known prophetic scene, described also in the Old Testament: "I will also gather all nations, and will bring them down into the valley of Jehoshaphat, and will plead with them there for my people and for my heritage Israel, whom they have scattered among the nations, and parted my land" (Joel 3:2). The purpose of this judgment is to determine which nations (Gentiles) shall enter the millennial kingdom prepared from the foundation of the world. Those which have been kind to the brethren of

Christ—"my heritage Israel"—will be invited to enter the kingdom. All others will be cast out. No nation appears to have a greater claim to this invitation than the United States. The Lord is going to judge America some day, but we are justified in hoping our country will be spared and that Americans will share the joy of the kingdom.

9. After the kingdom has been established, America will be ruled by the Lord Jesus Christ, King of kings and Lord of lords. "The kingdom is the Lord's: and he is the governor among the nations" (Ps. 22:28). Whatever form of national government prevails, it will be under the control of the Lord as the supreme world ruler. When God sets Christ as king on his holy hill of Zion, he will be given the nations for his inheritance and the uttermost parts of the earth as his possession (Ps. 2:6-8). Tolerating no interference with his righteous reign, he will "rule all nations with a rod of iron" (Rev. 12:5). America's armed forces will no longer be needed, for Christ will make wars to cease unto the end of the earth (Ps. 46:9). "They shall beat their swords into plowshares, and their spears into pruninghooks" (Isa. 2:4).

10. Impossible though it may seem today, America will call the Lord blessed during the thousand year reign of the Messiah (Ps. 72:17). False cults and religions will be no more. America will join other nations in going to the Lord's house in Jerusalem to learn of his ways in order to walk in his paths. "Out of Zion shall go forth the law, and the word of the Lord from Jerusalem" (Isa. 2:3).

When Christ's kingdom has run its course, the history of the saved nations of the millennium will be carried on into eternity. After the heavenly city, the new Jerusalem, comes down from God out of heaven, "the nations of them which are saved shall walk in the light of it: . . . and they shall bring the glory and honour of the nations into it" (Rev. 21:24, 26).

These examples of what the prophets have to say about the future of the nations, including that of the United States, begin with the rapture of the church. The world will pass through terrible days before earth's golden age dawns. If this strikes fear into the hearts of some, there is great comfort to be found in something the prophet Joel wrote twenty-eight hundred years ago: "Before the great and the terrible day of the Lord come, . . . whosoever shall call on the name of the Lord shall be delivered" (Joel 2:31, 32). We live in the period before that day of divine wrath is to begin. The word "whosoever" means us. Joel's words are quoted in Romans 10:13, one of the most memorized gospel texts. We need only call on the name of the Lord for salvation. He will deliver us from tribulation. No one need perish. Anyone may heed the call of God, put his trust in Christ, and escape the terrible day of the Lord.

CHAPTER 8
THE DESTRUCTION
OF RUSSIA

Russia is apparently named in the Bible. It is mentioned in a lengthy prophecy that describes its invasion of Israel in the last days and its destruction in a manner so appalling as to astonish the world. This mention of Russia is not generally known due to a curious error in the Authorized translation of Ezekiel 38:2, 3, which reads, "Son of man, set thy face against Gog, the land of Magog, the chief prince of Meshech and Tubal, and prophesy against him, and say, Thus saith the Lord God: Behold, I am against thee, O Gog, the chief prince of Meshech and Tubal."

When the King James Version of the Bible was being prepared in 1611, a proper name, Rosh, was found in the Hebrew text. This name is associated with two other proper names, Meshech and Tubal. No nation bearing the name Rosh was known to antiquity. Thus the translators rendered the name Rosh as "chief." This was one of the meanings of the original root. In so doing they departed from the precedent set by the seventy scholars who translated the Septuagint Version of the Old Testament, a Greek translation of the Hebrew made in Alexandria 250 years before Christ. The Revised Versions of 1881 and 1901 correctly followed the example of the Septuagint by changing the phrase to read, "the prince of Rosh, Meshech and Tubal."

Some modern translations have retained the error of the Authorized Version, but it is clear that Ezekiel wrote of three nations, not two, as he gave us his prophecy of the end times.

There is to be a man named Gog, the prince of Rosh, leading an invasion of Palestine in the last days. Is Rosh Russia? There is an astonishing explanation of the source of the name "Russia," which even several Soviet scholars accept. When barbarians from the north invaded the Byzantine Empire in the ninth century, the patriarch Photius in Constantinople called them Ros, identifying them with the invaders of Ezekiel 38. The name came to be widely applied to the aggressors. It passed from the Greek language into the Russian, underwent a spelling change, and emerged as the name of the nation Russia. The name "Russia" first appeared in a document dated A.D. 839. God has branded a prominent twentieth-century country with the name he gave it through his prophet over one thousand years before that date.

The names of the two peoples associated with Rosh are in agreement with this. Meshech and Tubal appear in the ancient table of the nations as sons of Japheth and brothers of Gomer (Gen. 10:2). They were the progenitors of warlike tribes living in the far north. It is possible that these two words have been preserved in the names of two Russian rivers, the Moskva, on which Moscow is located, and the Tobol, from which the city of Tobolsk took its name.

Whether or not Rosh is an ancient name for Russia, that nation does occupy the region to the far north of the land of Israel. Moscow is directly north of Jerusalem. That is the direction from which an invasion is to come some day, like the invasions of the Assyrians and the Babylonians. God asked Jeremiah, "What seest thou?" and the prophet replied, "I see a seething pot; and the face thereof is toward the north. Then the Lord said unto me, Out of the north an evil shall break forth upon all the inhabitants of the land" (Jer. 1:13, 14). "Thus saith the Lord, Behold, a people cometh from the north country, and a great nation shall be raised up from the sides of the earth. They shall lay hold on bow and spear; they are cruel, and have no mercy; their voice roareth like the sea; and they ride upon horses, set in array as men of war against thee, O daughter of Zion" (6:22, 23).

Gog is the prince who leads the attack, Magog is his land. The heights of the Caucusus mountains have long been known as "Gogh." The identities of other nations associated with Gog in his invasion of the Holy Land are most interesting. The "Persia" of Ezekiel 38:5 is modern Iran. Ethiopia is south of Egypt, Libya is west of Egypt on the Mediterranean coast. Gomer's descendants occupied the territory of present day Germany. Gomer had a son named Ashkenaz (Gen. 10:3); German Jews have been called Askenazim for centuries. The words "Gomer and all his bands" possibly refer to the many Germanic bands united into one nation by Bismarck. If these identifications are correct, the confederacy headed by the prince of Rosh will include Middle Eastern, African, and European countries.

Five times in Ezekiel's prophecy we find the phrase, "and many people with thee" (e.g., Ezek. 38:6). It has been suggested that these people may come from the populous lands of the east, because other areas of the world are specifically mentioned elsewhere in descriptions of the last days. Furthermore, eastern nations are to participate in Armageddon (Rev. 16:12-16). Because of these texts, Bible students in the nineteenth century expected China would some day become confederate with Russia.

According to Ezekiel, the invaders come "to take a spoil, and to take a prey" (Ezek. 38:12). A parallel passage in Joel refers to a desire for conquest, in the words of the prayer, "Give not thine heritage to reproach, that the heathen should rule over them" (Joel 3:17). Further light on why these events take place is found in Zechariah's revelation about Jerusalem becoming "a cup of trembling" and "a burdensome stone" (a source of international trouble) in the end times (Zech. 12:2, 3).

Russia's action will result in protests by other nations, but there will be no active intervention. "Sheba, and Dedan, and the merchants of Tarshish, with all the young lions thereof, shall say unto thee, Art thou come to take a spoil? hast thou gathered thy company to take a prey?" (Ezek. 38:13). Sheba and Dedan were nations occupying Arabia when this prophecy was written. Tarshish may have been Tartessus, which lies west of Gibraltar in Spain. Some have identified Tarshish as England, claiming "the young lions" are such colonies as America (obviously, this suggestion is based on extremely tenuous grounds). Sheba and Tarshish are mentioned as existing during the millennial kingdom (Ps. 72:10).

There is a disagreement as to the exact timing of the invasion Ezekiel prophesied; no specific revelation is given. It will be "after many days . . . in the latter years . . . in the latter days" (Ezek. 38:8, 16). Some details have been cited to show it may come early in the kingdom age, but the Lord is going to cast out "all things that offend, and them which do iniquity" when he *begins* his reign (Matt. 13:41). For different reasons, it has been suggested that Russia will come against Israel in the closing days of the church age. Most scholars agree that Ezekiel was writing about the seven years of tribulation which precede Christ's second coming. Those who favor the middle of that period point to the fact the Jews will be dwelling safely in unwalled ("open," lit.,) villages, which may mean the Jews are under the protection of the Antichrist after a treaty with him has been signed (Dan. 9:27). Some think the destruction of the northern confederacy may provide the opportunity for the beast to become a world ruler, since his greatest enemy will have been disposed of.

Others would place the invasion during the latter part of the tribulation, not long before Armageddon. After God intervenes, the people will recognize him as the Jehovah of Old Testament days and turn to him. He will pour out his Spirit and bless them. Never again will they pollute his name (Ezek. 39:7). These revelations seem to require that the events of Ezekiel 38 take place before the Spirit is outpoured at the second coming of Christ (Ezek. 39:29; Zech. 12:10).

It has recently been suggested that in this passage Ezekiel is describing Armageddon itself. If this were true, it would solve the problem of just when Russia and her allies invade the land. However, the text does not permit this solution. In Ezekiel Gog is the leader, while at Armageddon the Antichrist dominates the scene. A limited confederacy of nations is described by the prophet, while all nations are involved at Armageddon. Divine intervention in Ezekiel takes the form of natural phenomena like pestilence and earthquake, while the Antichrist is to be destroyed by the Lord himself. No battles are mentioned at the time of the invasion from the north, while Armageddon is to bring warfare such as the world has never known.

It is significant that the invasion of Ezekiel 38 is placed between a regathering of the people of Israel (chapters 36 and 37) and the establishing of the kingdom of the Messiah (chapters 40-48). A return to the land in unbelief is possibly referred to in the story of the valley of dry bones: "There was no breath in them" (37:8). There is no question, however, that the main point of the story in Ezekiel 37 is that God will someday restore the Jews to their land.

Gog and his armies will come up against the Jews who are "gathered out of the nations" (Ezek. 38:12). This gathering could refer to the present return. It is not said to be the result of divine activity, as is that of 39:27: "When I have brought them again from the people, and gathered them out of their enemies' lands. . . ."

Ezekiel reveals that no Jewish army will confront the enemy and no allies will come to Israel's aid. The only action against the prince of Rosh will come from God, whose fury and wrath are manifested when his land is invaded. He will take up the same weapons he used to defend his people in the Old Testament. The first of these is an earthquake: "There shall be a great shaking in the land of Israel; . . . the mountains shall be thrown down, and every wall shall fall to the ground" (Ezek. 38:19, 20). God used this weapon when Jonathan went out against the Philistines near Gibeah, when "the earth quaked" (1 Sam. 14:15).

God will also call for a sword against the enemy throughout all his mountains. "Every man's sword shall be against his brother" (Ezek. 38:21). When Gideon's chosen three hundred men blew their trumpets, "the Lord set every man's sword against his fellow" (Judg. 7:22) and the Midianites were driven away. There is a third divine weapon. God says, "I will plead against him with pestilence and with blood" (Ezek. 38:22). This is a reminder of the time when a plague killed 185,000 Assyrians who were besieging Jerusalem (2 Kings 19:35).

A fourth weapon will be "an overflowing rain, and great hailstones" (Ezek. 38:22). The tremendous destructive power of these was seen when God saved the Jews from the Amorites in the days of Joshua: "They were more which died with hailstones than they whom the children of Israel slew with the sword" (Josh. 10:11). Hailstones are also mentioned in Revelation 16:21 when the seventh vial of the wrath of God is poured on the earth. Finally, fire and brimstone are mentioned in the arsenal of weapons used against Gog, as when the Lord destroyed Sodom and Gomorrah (Gen. 19:24). God will send fire on Magog, the land from which the invading hosts have come (Ezek. 39:6).

The world will view this destruction of the armies of Rosh. Many nations will recognize the destruction as an act of God in defense of his land (Ezek. 38:23). When God turns back the northern confederacy, five-sixths of the vast host will lie dead on the mountains of Israel (39:2). "And seven months shall the house of Israel be burying of them, that they may cleanse the land" (39:12). Burial crews will search for human bones after the seven months. Travelers passing through the land will place a marker near every bone left behind by scavenging animals and birds. The employment of such special burial crews has led some to speculate that nuclear weapons may be used to defeat the confederacy.

A valley is to be set aside as a burial place for the northern armies. It will be called the valley of *Hamon-Gog* ("the multitude of Gog"). The people that come to find spoil will find a place of graves instead. Somewhere near the valley will be a city, Hamonah ("the multitude"), a memorial of these strange events. The Septuagint says the burial valley will be closed off with a wall. This valley of bones matches the valley of dry bones of Ezekiel 37.

The most difficult question about this prophecy concerns the weaponry of the invaders. It is usually assumed that we cannnot take Ezekiel's language literally, because he speaks of such things as bows, arrows, and spears. Some would alter the text by substituting what are called "equivalent words" when the text is applied to the last days. These people change inspired language on the theory that the prophet used the terminology of a bygone era, and that it could not possibly apply to a modern army. This, of course, is a denial of the doctrine of verbal inspiration. To escape this problem, some have suggested Ezekiel was writing of a time so far in the distant future that men will have forgotten how to make guns, and will have to reinvent the bow and arrow.

A far simpler explanation is possible: Hebrew is a language of word pictures. Words are often descriptions of the things they refer to. "Dog" translated literally is "a barker." A fox is "a burrower"; a sparrow is "a hopper"; a serpent is "a hisser." The sun is "the shining one," a palm tree is "the straight or erect one." Similar words in English are not easy to find. They include such descriptive terms as woodpecker, flyer, rower, and flamethrower.

The invaders are said to have horses (Ezek. 38:4). The Hebrew word for horse is *sus*, meaning something which leaps forward—"a leaper." The original root is also used of birds in Isaiah 38:14. It is a word picture of something which propels itself forward over the ground or through the air. The word translated "horsemen" may refer to riders on horses, or to drivers of wheeled vehicles such as the chariots of Exodus 14:28. The word translated "sword" is literally a cutting or destroying instrument, the word for "arrow" means a piercing missile, and the word for "bow" means a launching device for such a missile. All these words meant something specific and familiar to the people of Ezekiel's day.

When this passage is read as a description of weapons used by armies in the last days before the Lord returns, it is not necessary to attach the ancient meanings to these word pictures. For example, we need not translate Ezekiel 39:3 as it is rendered in the Authorized Version: "And I will smite thy bow out of thy left hand, and will cause thine arrows to fall out of thy right hand." If we use the word pictures instead of what was meant in ancient times, the verse translates, "And I will smite thy launcher out of thy left hand, and will cause thy missiles to fall out of thy right hand." Such a translation is free of the problems presented by insisting these Hebrew words be translated today as they were in Ezekiel's time. The word pictures can describe modern weapons just as accurately as they described those in use twenty-five hundred years ago.

What is true of the bows and arrows of this prophecy is true of other words. A *sus* was a horse in Ezekiel; it may refer to a different kind of "leaper" when it is used of the latter days. The word translated "shield" was something that protected its user. The same word is used of the scales or protective hide of a crocodile in Job 41:15. The Hebrew word translated "buckler" comes from a root meaning "prickly" or "sharp." It is translated "hooks" in Amos 4:2. A "hand stave" was an object held in the hand, such as a rod, but the Hebrew root means "to germinate" or "to shoot forth." Gesenius renders the word as "dart" or "javelin" in Ezekiel 39:9. The word translated "spear" was something thrown or hurled. It may be rendered "projectile," and it might refer to a hand grenade, or some similar weapon.

The people from the cities of Israel will gather the weapons of the northern armies and burn them for fuel. Some have imagined this calls for immense piles of wooden bows, arrows, and spears, but the Hebrew word for "weapons" is simply "military equipment." In modern warfare it would include vast quantities of combustible fuel. It is perfectly reasonable that such fuel, sufficient for large armies, could supply the decimated population of Israel for seven years (Ezek. 39:9), to say nothing of the individual pieces of equipment described only by word pictures.

In recent years a Dutch invention aroused great interest because of this particular text. By impregnating wood with certain chemicals and subjecting it to great pressure, a substance called lignostone was produced. It was found to be useful as a replacement for steel in heavy machinery and parts of some weapons, and it was combustible. It was suggested that weapons made of such a material could be burned as fuel, fulfilling Ezekiel's prophecy.

Several phrases in Ezekiel 38 have given rise to the notion that the prophet foretold the use of aircraft. The invaders will "ascend and come like a storm" (38:9), they will be "as a cloud to cover the land" (38:9), and they will "fall upon the mountains of Israel" (39:4). But such speculation does not take into account other uses in Scripture of the same terminology. Joshua's men ascended into the city when they took Jericho (Josh. 6:5). Men fell on the open field in battles long before airplanes were invented (Ezek. 39:5).

When body armor began to be used by modern soldiers, some thought this was a fulfillment of Ezekiel 38:4. The invading armies are described as "clothed in all sorts of armour." However, the word "armour" is in italics, because it is not found in the original Hebrew. What Ezekiel actually wrote was, "all of them clothed in all sorts. . . . " He did not finish his statement, as though no words were available to him to tell us what he saw. There was something so strange in his vision that it could not be portrayed in the vocabulary of that age.

It is evident that God could have prevented this invasion, had he chosen to do so. Instead, God is quoted as saying to the prince of Rosh, "I will bring thee against my land" (Ezek. 38:16). Why should Ezekiel say God will be behind the attack? The answer is given immediately: "That the heathen may know me, when I shall be sanctified in thee, O Gog, before their eyes." Five similar statements appear in the text.

Various Scriptures explain these statements. "When thy judgments are in the earth, the inhabitants of the world will learn righteousness" (Isa. 26:9). God is "not willing that any should perish, but that all should come to repentance" (2 Pet. 3:9). Such passages are keys to the history of mankind. When the armies of Rosh invade Israel, time will be running out for the human race. The opportunity for men to be saved and to have a part in the millennial kingdom of Christ will soon be over. Yet vast numbers will still be in rebellion against God, refusing his message of deliverance and failing to repent when the vials of his wrath are poured out (Rev. 16:9, 11). God has "no pleasure in the death of the wicked" (Ezek. 33:11). He has sought the salvation of men throughout the ages, showing his longsuffering by withholding judgment on the ungodly in order that all may have the chance to be saved.

Ezekiel reveals that God will give the world a demonstration of his wrath when godless armies come against his land. God will destroy them for the express purpose of causing the nations to know him. This is the true reason the invasion will take place. God will seek the salvation of men for one last time before the end. All the nations will see what he has done to Russia and its allies, and they will know he is God.

Ezekiel gives us a clue to when these events will take place: "The house of Israel shall know that I am the Lord their God from that day forward" (Ezek. 39:22). This passage does not say the Jews will recognize Christ at that time. They will, however, believe that the Jehovah of the Old Testament is indeed God. Eventually they will come to believe in Jesus (Zech. 12:9, 10).

The prophecy closes with a summary of God's activity on behalf of the Jews. The Lord will have mercy on the house of Israel. He will bring them back to the land, leaving none of them among the nations (Ezek. 39:28). Forgetting their evil years, they will live securely in their ancient land. God's face will no longer be hidden. The Holy Spirit will be poured out on all flesh.

Like pieces in a giant jigsaw puzzle, the events in the prophecy, written twenty-five hundred years ago, fit into the grand pattern of the divine program. They illuminate the days in which we live. Russia has become a world power, allied with some of the nations mentioned by Ezekiel. The rise of Gog may not be far away.

CHAPTER 9
THE COMING DICTATOR OF THE WORLD

The evil being who will dominate the world in the last days is mentioned many times throughout the Bible. He is introduced in the third chapter from the beginning of the Word, and he is mentioned for the last time in the third chapter from the end. In the first prophecy to be found in Scripture, God said to Satan, "I will put enmity between thee and the woman, and between thy seed and her seed; it shall bruise thy head, and thou shalt bruise his heel" (Gen. 3:15). These words contain the first mention of Christ. He is the Seed of the woman; his great final opponent is the seed of the serpent. The text contains a veiled reference to the death of Christ and the ultimate defeat of Satan.

Scores of passages between the first and last references to this personage tell of his appearance in the last days, his career, and his final doom. He will be wicked, a hater of God and his people, the embodiment of satanic wisdom and power. He is given many names. The prophet Daniel calls him the "king of fierce countenance," the "prince that shall come," and the "willful king." The apostle Paul adds the terms "the man of sin," "the son of perdition," and "the lawless one." He is the Antichrist of First John. He is called the "beast" thirty-six times in the Book of Revelation, a world dictator whom Christ will ultimately destroy.

The Bible describes the seed of the serpent in a progressive manner. From the first brief reference in Genesis, the theme is developed throughout the Old Testament. He appears in the teaching of Christ in the Gospels. The New Testament epistles tell us how he relates to the Holy Spirit, the church, and the present age. The picture is completed in Revelation, which sets forth his origin, character, relationship to the devil, domination of the world, and dreadful fate.

The apostles and the church fathers produced a considerable amount of literature on the Antichrist. Books and articles have continued to appear throughout every period of church history. As Christians we cannot ignore what the Spirit has revealed about this prophetic theme: "If any man have an ear, let him hear" (Rev. 13:9).

The coming world dictator will be a man, a fact the Bible emphasizes. He is called the man of sin, a prince, and a king. He will receive a deadly wound by a sword, and will then be "miraculously" healed. He will sit in the temple of God, speaking blasphemy. He will act according to his own will. He will sign a treaty with Israel, and will be worshipped. He will finally be defeated in battle and cast into the lake of fire, where he will suffer torment. A number is given to him, "the number of a man" (Rev. 13:18).

In spite of such clear revelations, during the Middle Ages it was popular to think of the coming beast as an evil principle or false religious system rather than an individual. Some identified the beast as Catholicism, others as Protestantism, later on as Islam. More recently the opinion has been expressed that he is communism, fascism, or even a computer! In the early church the common understanding of the fathers was that the Antichrist would be a man, indwelt by Satan and possessing supernatural powers.

Two statements in Revelation seem to make it evident that the beast is to be a Gentile. John wrote, "And I stood upon the sand of the sea, and saw a beast rise up out of the sea" (Rev. 13:1). This symbol of the sea may refer to the Gentile nations. "The waters which thou sawest, where the whore sitteth, are peoples, and multitudes, and nations, and tongues" (17:15). Daniel also had a vision of beasts coming up from the sea (Dan. 7:3). If the sea is indeed a symbol of the nations, in contrast with the earth, or land, from which the false prophet comes (presumably a Jew, Rev. 13:11), then the future world ruler will be a Gentile, not a Jew.

A clear indication of his national origin is found in Daniel's prediction: "The people of the prince that shall come shall destroy the city and the sanctuary" (Dan. 9:26). Daniel was writing about the destruction of Jerusalem and its temple by soldiers of the Roman Empire; this took place in A.D. 70. Since these were the people of the prince who is to come, the Antichrist will evidently come from the area occupied by the old Roman Empire. A western confederacy of nations will be in control of that region in the last days, and he will be its ruler. This would seem to make him a Gentile. He may first arise in the Near East, for the "little horn" of Daniel 8:9 represents the Antichrist. Antiochus Epiphanes came out of Syria to fulfill Daniel's prophecy. Syria was a part of the Empire, and that is also where the prince of Tyre came from. This prince was representative of the coming prince. The Assyrian of Isaiah 14:25 likewise came from that area.

When will the future world dictator appear? Part of the answer to this question can be found in 2 Thessalonians 2:8: "And then shall that Wicked be revealed, whom the Lord shall consume with the spirit of his mouth, and shall destroy with the brightness of his coming." The time word "then" is important. It refers back to certain events which must take place before the wicked one is revealed. Second Thessalonians 2:3 speaks of "a falling away first" ("the apostasy"). Next, he who now restrains iniquity or lawlessness will be removed from the scene. The restrainer is generally understood to be the Holy Spirit, dwelling in the church and holding back evil in the world. Not until the apostasy has come, and the Holy Spirit has departed to present the church to Christ as his bride (2 Cor. 4:14), will the Antichrist be revealed. Daniel places his appearance "in the latter time" (Dan. 8:23). Because of the time word "then" in 2 Thessalonians 2:8, it is useless to try to identify this evil being today as some existing political leader. After he finally appears on the scene, and exercises his power for a short time, Christ will destroy him.

Daniel describes how and when this world dictator arrives on the scene. In the last days ten kings will rule over the part of the world once occupied by the old Roman Empire. Another king will appear who will subdue three of the ten with violence (Dan. 7:8, 24). The conquest of these three nations will be the first recognizable indication that the Antichrist has appeared on the scene.

Of all the many names given to this evil being, none has taken hold of the popular imagination like Antichrist. Yet this title is applied to an individual only once in the Bible: "Ye have heard that antichrist shall come" (1 John 2:18). In popular usage it belongs to the first beast of Revelation 13:1, who rises from the sea, although some believe the title should be used of the second beast who rises from the land and becomes a religious leader (13:11, 12). But whether we call the political leader or the false prophet who serves him the Antichrist is a matter of personal preference, not scriptural accuracy. The word itself can mean either someone who is against Christ or someone who is a false Christ. It is customary today to think of him as an opponent of Christ rather than a counterfeit Messiah.

Soon after the beast is described in Revelation, an important key is given to his entire career: "The dragon gave him his power, and his seat, and great authority" (Rev. 13:2). As the text develops this subject, an evil trinity emerges, a perverse copy of the Holy Trinity. Satan has always wanted to be like God. He has said, "I will be like the most High" (Isa. 14:14). His greatest opportunity will come when he is cast into the earth during the great tribulation and receives the worship of the whole world as though he were God the Father. In imitation of the Son of God who will one day rule the earth as King of kings, the devil will have his chosen man, the beast, to become a temporary world dictator. The third member of the evil trinity will be the false prophet, who will direct all worship toward the beast and the devil, in imitation of the Holy Spirit who now glorifies Christ.

Over the centuries when great leaders such as Napoleon and Hitler have commanded world attention, Christians have wondered whether such men might not be rehearsals staged by Satan in preparation for the coming drama when the Antichrist will take the center of the stage and rule the world with all the accumulated wisdom and experience of the ages at his command. Sometimes individuals have so deeply impressed Christians with their likeness to Satan's beast that they have been widely believed to be the Antichrist himself. Two men in particular have been thus singled out as likely candidates— Nero and Judas.

There was a widespread belief in the early church that Nero would rise from the dead as the Antichrist, for prophecy says the beast is to ascend from the bottomless pit, or abyss, as though he were a man who lived before (Rev. 11:7; 17:8). Nero was regarded as the epitome of wickedness and cruelty.

In present times, some are convinced that Judas will appear on the earth again as Satan's beast. Reasons for this belief include the fact that Judas is the only individual who is called "a devil" (John 6:70), and the only one called "the son of perdition" (17:12). Satan entered into him while he was living (Luke 22:3). After he died he went "to his own place" (Acts 1:25), presumed to be the abyss. This abyss, or bottomless pit, is the place where demons are imprisoned (Rev. 9:1-21), and where Satan will be bound during the kingdom age (Rev. 20:1-3). The greatest difficulty with this view is that the beast will receive his deadly wound from a sword. Judas, as we know, committed suicide by hanging himself.

It is mentioned three times that the beast will receive a deadly wound (Rev. 13:3, 12, 14). When he is healed and lives, the whole world is awed and begins to worship him. In view of the fact that the whole world witnesses this miracle, the question has been raised as to whether such a thing could have happened before the advent of television and communication satellites.

Some commentaries insist that these texts about the wounding of the beast refer to the Roman Empire, not to the beast as a man. They say that the Empire perished, but is to be "resurrected" and will appear on the earth in a new form prior to Christ's second advent. But if this view is correct, it is difficult to understand why the whole world should be awed by, and then worship, a political empire simply because it had a counterpart hundreds of years before. The simplest explanation of these passages is that they speak of the wounding of a man, and of his healing by satanic power.

The actual career of the beast as the Antichrist begins with this miracle. It is the first thing written about him after the dragon is cast down and gives him his power. The beast will have ruled the western confederacy of ten nations already for three and a half years when it happens. A number of events are mentioned together in the text as though they are closely related.

When the great tribulation begins, Satan will be cast down from heaven to earth, and the persecution of the Jews, called "the time of Jacob's trouble" (Jer. 30:7; Rev. 12:9-13), will ensue. The beast will receive a deadly or fatal wound by a sword, but will not die. He will receive power, a throne, and great authority from the devil (13:1-3). He then will break the treaty he had previously signed with Israel. This will take place at the middle of the final seven years (Dan. 9:27). The abomination of desolation will be put in the holy place (Matt. 24:15). God's two witnesses will be killed (Rev. 11:7). Some would place the destruction of the Soviet Union at this same time, believing it opens the way for the beast to become a world ruler (Ezek. 38, 39).

The Antichrist will institute three remarkable international systems during the forty-two months following the beginning of Satan's control of him. First, he will introduce a world government: "Power was given him over all kindreds, and tongues, and nations" (Rev. 13:7). Old Testament prophecy declares his empire will "devour the whole earth, and shall tread it down, and break it in pieces" (Dan. 7:23). This is a reference to both ancient Rome and the final world power destined to take its place under the Antichrist. The rhetorical question, "Who is able to make war with him?" (Rev. 13:4), is understandable because he will control all weapons. As dictator, he will act according to his own will, and prosper until his day is over (Dan. 8:24; 11:36). He will seek to change established laws (7:25).

When the end of his rule approaches, trouble will develop. It will come from three directions. As his control of the nations weakens, "the king of the south" and "the king of the north" will rebel. When he enters Palestine to crush these opponents, tidings out of the east and out of the north will trouble him (Dan. 11:40-45). The mention of the east is doubtless a reference to the approach of the armies of "the kings of the east" (Rev. 16:12). The Antichrist will go forth with great fury to destroy his opponents. Armageddon will be at hand.

Second, the beast will introduce a world religion: "All that dwell upon the earth shall worship him" except for those whose names are in the book of life (Rev. 13:8). These bear the seal of God, or believe God's message of deliverance proclaimed universally during the rule of the beast. The new system of worship will replace the ecumenical religious system called Mystery Babylon which will have taken over the world after the rapture. After being empowered by the devil, he will destroy Babylon and demand for himself and for Satan universal worship. In this he will have the help of the second beast of Revelation 13, a powerful religious leader who will order an image made of the first beast. All will be required to worship it under threat of death, in a remarkable parallel to the image worship required by the first great world ruler, Nebuchadnezzar (Dan. 3:1-7). Strange and terrible powers will be given to the image. It will breathe and be able to kill all who refuse to worship it (Rev. 13:14, 15). At some time during his career the beast will sit in the temple of God, showing himself that he is God (2 Thess. 2:4).

Third, the Antichrist will introduce a world economy. His false prophet "causeth all, both small and great, rich and poor, free and bond, to receive a mark in their right hand, or in their foreheads: and that no man might buy or sell, save he that had the mark, or the name of the beast, or the number of his name" (Rev. 13:16, 17). The number of the beast is the number of a man, "and his number is Six hundred threescore and six" (13:18).

Attempts have been made for centuries to make the letters of the names of great leaders equal 666, by using the Hebrew, Greek, or Roman alphabets, which have numerical equivalents. Some of these exercises in futility have been quite ridiculous. There have been so many of them as to make it clear that God does not want anyone to know the true meaning of the mystic number until the beast has finally appeared.

The beast will openly oppose the God of the Bible. "[He] shall speak marvellous things against the God of gods" (Dan. 11:36). "He opened his mouth in blasphemy against God, to blaspheme his name, and his tabernacle, and them that dwell in heaven" (Rev. 13:6). The latter will include all who belong to the true church. Heaven will be their dwelling place after the rapture. This antagonism to God and all he stands for will also be evidenced by the fact that "craft" (or fraud) will prosper in those days—deceitful people will hold the advantage (Dan. 8:25).

At the beginning of the beast's control of the ten-nation confederacy, it will be to his advantage to befriend the nation of Israel. A treaty will be drawn up, perhaps guaranteeing for seven years the security of the land. After Satan takes full control of the beast, he will break the treaty, put a stop to the daily sacrifices being offered in the temple at Jerusalem, and begin the persecution of the people of Israel. The Jews will flee for their lives to the wilderness, where God will take care of them (Matt. 24:16). The devil will make war with all Jewish people who "keep the commandments of God, and have the testimony of Jesus Christ" (Rev. 12:17), a reference to those faithful Jews who proclaim or accept the good news about the Lord after the rapture has taken place (cf. Deut. 30:2).

The final end of the beast will be unimaginably horrible. Other wicked individuals have died dreadful deaths by being swallowed alive by the earth, burned by fire sent from the Lord, hanged, smitten with disease, or eaten by dogs and worms. But only the Antichrist will be "broken without hand" by the Prince of princes (Dan. 8:25). He will be consumed by the spirit of Christ's mouth and destroyed with the brightness of Christ's coming (2 Thess. 2:8).

Zechariah prophesies that the armies of all the nations will be gathered against Jerusalem as Armageddon climaxes the wars of the ages. Christ will "touch down" on the Mount of Olives, just east of Jerusalem. The Book of Revelation depicts the opening of heaven and the descent of Jesus Christ with all his armies. On his clothing and on his thigh a name will be written: "King of kings, and Lord of lords." An angel will call together the fowls of the skies to eat the flesh of the assembled armies. Christ will take the beast and the false prophet. The two beasts will be cast alive into a lake of fire burning with brimstone (Rev. 19:11-20).

With the end of the beast, and the end of Armageddon, the invisible war of the ages will be over at last. Christ will judge the Gentiles still living, regather his ancient people Israel, and establish his kingdom on the earth. The millennium will begin.

CHAPTER 10
ARMAGEDDON

The battle of Armageddon is one of the most discussed subjects of Bible prophecy, yet this expression does not appear in Scripture. In the only place where the word is found, the kings of the earth are gathered together to "a place called in the Hebrew tongue Armageddon" (Rev. 16:16). The purpose of their gathering is for "the battle of that great day of God Almighty" (16:14). The text does not say the battle (lit., war) will be fought at that place. Parallel passages show that the entire land is to be involved in a final great conflict.

Armageddon means "Mount of Megiddo" in the original Greek. Most evangelical commentators understand it as a reference to the heights overlooking the site of the ancient city of Megiddo, on the plain of Esdraelon, sixty miles north of Jerusalem. The Old Testament speaks of the valley of Megiddo, the city and its towns, and the waters of Megiddo, a stream flowing into the river Kishon. The mount itself, sometimes called the acropolis of the city, is not mentioned. The Hebrew root of the name is usually given as "slaughter," or "a cutting off." The place is well named; over the years great numbers of men have perished there in battle. "Hardly an equal area of earth can so often have been drenched with the blood of men" (*International Standard Bible Encyclopedia*, Eerdman's, 1930).

There are compelling reasons to interpret Revelation 16:16 literally. The Mount of Megiddo dominates the greatest plain in Israel. This plain has been the stage for many battles. It was

Israel's main field of battle with invaders. Israel won two outstanding victories there, when Barak defeated the Canaanites and when Gideon overcame the Midianites (Judg. 4, 5, 7).

Today the plain is named Esdraelon. This name is not mentioned in the Bible, but it appears in the Apocrypha (Judith 3:9) as the Greek equivalent for the ancient valley of Jezreel (see Judg. 6:33). Jezreel was originally the name of the valley adjacent to the city of Jezreel near Mt. Gilboa. Later the name was used to refer to the entire plain now known as Esdraelon. It extends from the Mediterranean Sea to the Jordan valley, in the form of a rough triangle, separating the mountains of Carmel and Samaria from those of Galilee. Two of the plain's borders are each fifteen miles long, and the third side extends for twenty miles. Springs water the valley in three places. The springs of Megiddo produced extensive marshes until the Jews drained them to make way for farmland. One eastern spring still bears the name "Gideon's fountain." The river Kishon flows from the plain into the Mediterranean Sea north of Mount Carmel.

Esdraelon is well known in military history. Israel not only won great victories there; it also suffered great defeats. That is where King Saul was killed (1 Sam. 31), and where King Josiah was mortally wounded in his battle with the Egyptians under Pharaoh Necho (2 Kings 23:29). The Crusaders were defeated near the Horns of Hattin in A.D. 1187. General Allenby was victorious over the Turks there in 1917; he was subsequently known as "Lord Allenby of Megiddo." In *The Battle of Megiddo* (Chicago, 1921 [Private edition distributed by University of Chicago]) Harold H. Nelson says the tactics of troop disposition can be examined for the first time in the records of a battle fought at Megiddo in 1479 between the confederate princes of Syria and Palestine on one side and Egypt on the other. Thus Armageddon, or Esdraelon, is a starting point for the study of the history of military science.

Esdraelon has an unusual history. On that plain the stars in their courses fought against Israel's enemies. The forces of nature were unleashed. A flash flood in the Kishon swept away the Canaanites. "The earth trembled, and the heavens dropped, the clouds also dropped water" (Judg. 5:4; see also 5:20, 21). In the days of Gideon a supernatural panic overtook the Midianites: "The Lord set every man's sword against his fellow, even throughout all the host" (7:22).

George Adam Smith wrote about this in *The Historical Geography of the Holy Land* (Collins-World, 1976):

> What a plain it is! Upon which not only the greatest empires, races and faiths, east and west, have contended with each other, but each has come to judgment—on which from the first, with all its splendor of human battle, men have felt that there was fighting from heaven, the stars in their courses were fighting—on which panic has descended so mysteriously upon the best equipped and most successful armies, but the humble have been exalted to victory in the hour of their weakness. (p. 409)

Some of what has been written about "the battle of Armageddon" is confusing. Great armies are sometimes pictured as fighting each other there, with no mention of who the adversaries are, or what they are fighting about, or why they have come to that place to do their fighting. The literal meaning of Revelation 16:14-16 is sometimes dismissed; in *The Revelation of Jesus Christ* (Moody, 1966), John F. Walvoord writes, "The area, though it is a large one, is not sufficient for the armies of all the world" (p. 239). If this were true, then we would have to reject Zechariah 14:2 which quotes the Lord as saying, "I will gather all nations against Jerusalem to battle." If the vast plain of Esdraelon is too small for the gathering of the kings, then what can be said about the rugged terrain around Jerusalem, where no such plain is to be found? The text of Revelation 16:16 says nothing about how large the forces gathered at Armageddon are going to be. When Napolean looked out over Esdraelon, he is reported to have said all the armies of the world could be gathered there.

To understand the events which will find their beginning

at Armageddon, it is necessary to examine several passages of Scripture in which God is associated with warfare on the earth at the time of the return of Christ. Armageddon will become prominent at "that great day of God Almighty." Out of all the references to a coming great day, only a few mention a battle, or a war. Most such passages emphasize some other aspect of what is often called "the day of the Lord." There is "the day of visitation" (1 Pet. 2:12); "the day of the Lord's wrath" (Zeph. 1:18); and "the day of his wrath" (Rev. 6:17). Angels will stand before God at "the judgment of the great day" (Jude 1:6).

Great preparations will be made for the day of Armageddon: "Prepare war, wake up the mighty men, let all the men of war draw near; let them come up: beat your plowshares into swords, and your pruninghooks into spears" (Joel 3:9, 10). The manufacture of munitions is to be followed by the assembling of all the nations, and at this time God's mighty ones will come down (3:11; Rev. 19:11-16). Heaven will open and Christ will appear, followed by the armies of heaven, to fight against the nations (Zech. 14:3).

This military assembly is referred to in several places. "My determination is to gather the nations, that I may assemble the kingdoms, to pour upon them mine indignation, even all my fierce anger" (Zeph. 3:8). God is behind this worldwide activity, but demonic forces are also at work, motivating the kings of the earth (Rev. 16:14). The Book of Revelation places Armageddon at a particular time in history: not until the devil, the beast, and the false prophet form an evil trinity at work in the world, will the nations gather for the great war. "The kings of the east" will cross the Euphrates (16:12) to meet with the other kings. The grand place of assembly for these forces is Mount Megiddo, from which the plain of Esdraelon stretches out to the horizon.

When we consider the total picture, it is clear Jerusalem will be the focal point for this world gathering. It is mentioned in four different passages (i.e., "I will gather all nations against Jerusalem to battle," Zech. 14:2). As the war develops, there will be bloodshed up and down the entire length of the land of Israel, a distance of 180 miles (Rev. 14:20). The Lord is described as coming from Edom with his garments stained with the blood of his enemies (Isa. 63:1-6). Many think that fighting among the kings will increase the fury of the war (Dan. 11:40).

The most specific time word in all these prophecies is found in Zechariah 14:2, 3. When Jerusalem falls and half its population is taken captive, *then* the sky will open and Christ will come forth with his mighty ones. He will arrive on the earth at the Mount of Olives, which overlooks Jerusalem from the east. An earthquake will change the topography of the land and of the whole world. Panic will break out among the besieging forces, as in ancient times (Zech. 14:13). Their leader, the beast, will be cast into the lake of fire. His armies will be slain. A comparison of Revelation 19:19-21 with Zechariah 14:16 makes it clear that some of the armies in other parts of the land will survive, for "every one that is left of all the nations which came against Jerusalem" will afterward worship the King.

One element in this final struggle is often ignored. The beast and his kings "make war with the Lamb" (Rev. 17:14). "And I saw the beast, and the kings of the earth, and their armies, gathered together to make war against him that sat on the horse, and against his army" (19:19). A parallel reference is Psalm 2:2, 3: "The kings of the earth set themselves, and the rulers take counsel together, against the Lord, and against his anointed, saying, Let us break their bands asunder, and cast away their cords from us."

This is the culmination of the invisible war of the ages. In the beginning God put enmity between the Seed of the woman and the seed of the serpent (Gen. 3:15). Those who serve Satan have always sought to defeat the purposes of God. They tried to destroy the line from which Christ was to come, they tried to kill Christ himself, and now they persecute his body, the church. That invisible battle will become open warfare at the time of the Lord's return. When he comes, "every eye shall see him" (Rev. 1:7). His coming will be as visible as a flash of lightning (Matt. 24:27). He will be in plain view as he descends from the sky.

It is difficult to understand how men could make war with the Lamb. The present generation has seen the development of air power, satellites, and nuclear weapons capable of striking targets thousands of miles away. Perhaps with these sophisticated weapons the beast and his forces will think they are capable of resisting the Lamb and his heavenly host. But he who sits in the heavens will laugh as the returning King of kings destroys them with the breath of his mouth.

CHAPTER 11
THE DESTINY
OF THE UNSAVED

The Bible separates mankind into two groups: the saved and the lost, or the just and the unjust, or the children of the kingdom and the children of the wicked one. The destiny of each group is outlined in detail throughout Scripture. The final end of the saved is glorious, while the final end of the lost or unsaved is tragic. Men tend to approve of the one destiny, but they attack what is written about the other. Heaven is taken for granted; hell is rejected as inconsistent with a God of mercy and love. But human opinion does not alter the fact that both are matters of divine revelation.

It is the gospel which divides men into these two groups. Life comes from believing what God has revealed about salvation; rejecting salvation leads to eternal doom. The apostle Paul defined the gospel, or good news, in concise terms: "I. declare unto you the gospel which I preached unto you. . . . Christ died for our sins according to the scriptures; . . . he was buried, and . . . rose again the third day according to the scriptures" (1 Cor. 15:1-4).

There are two attitudes toward these truths: "The preaching of the cross is to them that perish foolishness; but unto us which are saved it is the power of God" (1 Cor. 1:18); "He that believeth on him is not condemned: but he that believeth not is condemned already, because he hath not believed in the name of the only begotten Son of God" (John 3:18). Contrary to the popular notion that our eternal destiny will be determined in the distant future, judgment is a present reality. Everyone who has not believed God's Word is now condemned.

Scripture carries this twofold division all the way into eternity. In resurrection some will awake to everlasting life, others to "shame and everlasting contempt" (Dan. 12:2). Christ spoke of "the resurrection of life" and "the resurrection of damnation" (John 5:29). The Bible contains scores of statements about what lies between the death of unsaved people and the day of their resurrection.

Associated with this body of truth are a number of terms used to describe the unjust. For example, they are called ungodly, unholy, wicked, and the perishing. They are declared to be unworthy of everlasting life. The gospel is hidden from them: "If our gospel be hid, it is hid to them that are lost: in whom the god of this world hath blinded the minds of them which believe not, lest the light of the glorious gospel of Christ, who is the image of God, should shine unto them" (2 Cor. 4:3, 4). The eternal salvation of men is such an important part of God's plan that evil forces are strongly opposed to it. What is widely regarded as of little importance now will be seen in its true light when eternity has dawned and the bitter cry is heard, "The harvest is past, the summer is ended, and we are not saved" (Jer. 8:20).

Each Testament records a remarkable historical incident meant to show us what happens to unsaved people when they die. The Old Testament account is the story of Korah, a prince in Israel, who with other men rebelled against the leadership of Moses and Aaron. An entire chapter is devoted to it. The climax of the record occurs when Korah and his company are standing by themselves at some distance from Moses and the congregation of Israel. Suddenly "the ground clave asunder that was under them. And the earth opened her mouth, and swallowed them up, and their houses, and all the men that appertained unto Korah, and all their goods. They, and all that appertained to them, went down alive into the pit, and the earth closed upon them: and they perished from among the congregation" (Num. 16:31-33).

"The pit" into which these men plunged when the earth split open before them is *Sheol* in the original text, a word rendered "hell" thirty-one times in the Authorized Version. It is also translated "the grave" in many places, and "the pit" three times. The American Revised Version of 1901 renders the word simply "Sheol." Gesenius, the great Hebrew lexicographer, defines Sheol as "a cavity, a hollow subterranean place." Scripture says this place is located in the nether, or lower, parts of the earth. People descend or go down into it at death. God said of Pharaoh, "I cast him down to hell with them that descend into the pit" (Ezek. 31:16). Others who now occupy that place are Asshur, Elam, Meshech and Tubal, Edom, the princes of the north, the Sidonians, and the multitude of Egypt (32:18-32).

Sheol is described as deep (Job 11:8), insatiable (Isa. 5:14), and never full (Prov. 27:20). It is a secure prison, because it has bars (Job 17:16). It has an entrance (Isa. 5:14), gates (Isa. 38:10), and keys (Rev. 1:18). It is a place of suffering (Ps. 116:3) and a place of fire (Deut. 32:22). It is the destiny of all who die without having been saved: "The wicked shall be turned into hell [Sheol, lit.], and all the nations that forget God" (Ps. 9:17). In view of all that has been written about this underground prisonhouse of the lost, it is surprising how little is known about it.

What was Korah's sin, and why does this terrible account appear in the Bible? Korah and his associates were wicked men; their outstanding sin was to reject Moses, the mediator God had appointed to stand between himself and his sinful people. No one can approach God without a mediator, and "there is one God, and one mediator between God and man, the man Christ Jesus" (1 Tim. 2:5). In rejecting Moses, Korah became an example for posterity of what God does with all who are guilty of what is called "the gainsaying of [Korah]" in Jude 1:11. To gainsay means to deny or contradict. In the original text the word means standing against the Word.

Complementing this account of Korah's fate is the revelation that "the children of Korah died not" (Num. 26:11). They and their descendants continued to live among the people of God. Several Psalms were written "for the sons of Korah."

They contain what seem to be references to the fate of their ancestors: "My life draweth nigh unto the grave [Sheol, lit.]. I am counted with them that go down to the pit" (Ps. 88:3, 4); "God will redeem my soul from the power of the grave [Sheol, lit.]" (49:15). The disclosure that the children of Korah did not perish is in keeping with the divine principle of Deuteronomy 24:16: "Neither shall the children be put to death for the fathers: every man shall be put to death for his own sin."

The New Testament passage corresponding to the story of Korah is the account of the rich man and Lazarus found in Luke 16:19-31. Some people believe this is a parable, by which they usually mean an imaginary or fictitious story. But the Bible presents it as a true and trustworthy record about a particular rich man and a named beggar. Furthermore, it is inconceivable that Christ, "the faithful and true witness" (Rev. 3:14) would teach something his followers cannot accept as true and dependable in every detail.

In this account, both men died. Lazarus the beggar, a godly man, was carried by the angels to "Abraham's bosom," a Hebrew expression referring to paradise and the blessedness of intimate fellowship with departed saints. Lazarus then joined Abraham, the father of the faithful. The rich man also died, and his body was buried, but immediately he found himself in Hades, the Greek equivalent for the Hebrew Sheol (when Psalm 16:10 is quoted in Acts 2:27, Hades is used in place of Sheol). After death, the rich man was conscious and in full possession of his faculties. He was tormented by flame and longed for water. He could see Abraham, recognize him, and call to him for help, just as the Old Testament inhabitants of Sheol were able to speak out of the midst of the pit (Ezek. 32:21). The rich man remembered his life on earth.

Something of the horror of Sheol is revealed here when Abraham speaks about a great gulf fixed between him and the rich man, "so that they which would pass from hence to you cannot; neither can they pass to us, that would come from thence" (Luke 16:26). It is the consistent testimony of Scripture that eternal destiny is determined during the present life. Where a tree falls, there it lies (Eccles. 11:3). It is too late for any change after death has come. The rich man pleaded that his living brothers would surely make the right choice and escape Hades if someone could rise from the dead to warn them. Abraham's reply was, "If they hear not Moses and the prophets, neither will they be persuaded, though one rose from the dead" (Luke 16:31). Christ has risen from the dead, but men refuse to accept his warnings about the penalty for refusing salvation.

What is taught in Luke 16 is in perfect accord with what is written throughout the Bible about the unseen world. The English word "destruction," which appears more than ninety times in the Authorized Version, is used to translate thirty-seven different Hebrew and Greek words. Many of these original words describe the destiny of the unsaved, and many of them are prophetic, as in Psalm 55:23: "Thou, O God, shalt bring them down into the pit of destruction," or in Matthew 7:13 where Christ said, "Wide is the gate, and broad is the way, that leadeth to destruction, and many there be which go in thereat."

When the roots of these thirty-seven words are traced, a dreadful picture emerges of the true meaning of the KJV's "destruction": unsaved persons discover that a dreadful calamity has overtaken them when they die. They have been snared like birds in a net, and are unable to escape. They are said to be taken away, cast into the pit. They perish, they are cut off, ruined, consumed, ravaged, wasted. They are desolated, broken, lost. Their state is one of corruption and perdition, where they suffer pangs of bitterness, remorse, and torment. One word picture shows them shrinking in terror. Others depict confusion, an uproar, a tempest in which they wander aimlessly. In this entire list, there is not a single word suggesting annihilation. Unsaved people do not cease to exist after death. They live forever in the place of misery to which their unbelief has brought them, the temporary Sheol being ultimately replaced by what Revelation calls the lake of fire.

Any study of the destiny of the unsaved should include a discussion about what happens to the people who will be left behind after the rapture of the church. When in the twinkling of an eye every Christian vanishes from the sight of men, two kinds of people will remain—those who have heard and rejected the gospel, and those who have never heard. Scripture speaks of each group. Second Thessalonians 2:10-12 is the central passage dealing with persons who have refused to put their trust in Christ during the present age: "Because they received not the love of the truth, that they might be saved. And for this cause God shall send them strong delusion, that they should believe a lie: that they all might be damned who believed not the truth, but had pleasure in unrighteousness." After the rapture people who have heard and rejected the truth of the gospel will be supernaturally blinded to the truth and believe the lie of Antichrist. They will have no second chance. The terrors of the tribulation period will not drive them to God. Instead, they will be deceived by Satan's world ruler as he comes to power. It is a solemn thought that many of these individuals may be living on earth today, never realizing they may already have refused for the last time God's present offer of salvation.

There is another group of people who will be left behind by the rapture—those who never had the opportunity of hearing the gospel. But God will never leave the earth without a witness; after the church has been translated, the gospel of the kingdom will be preached in all the world (Matt. 24:14). With the missionaries of the church taken away to heaven, God's representatives at that time will be people chosen from the twelve tribes of Israel (Rev. 7:1-8). The gospel of the kingdom will be the announcement that the kingdom of heaven is at hand, as it was when Christ came the first time (Matt. 3:2; 4:23). It includes the message of the cross (Rev. 7:14).

The message will be rejected by those to whom God will have sent strong delusion, but many people will believe it. They will become the "saints" mentioned in Revelation. Those saints who survive the tribulation will enter the kingdom prepared from the foundation of the earth. They will form "a great multitude, which no man could number, of all nations, and kindreds, and people, and tongues" (Rev. 7:9). When the Lord comes, others will perish, but these will be saved. His coming will be "in flaming fire taking vengeance on them that know not God, and that obey not the gospel of our Lord Jesus Christ" (2 Thess. 1:8).

Sheol, or Hades, will continue to receive all unsaved persons who die until it is finally emptied after Christ's earthly kingdom has run its course. At that time the great white throne will be set up for the judgment of the dead of all ages.

Several major themes often mentioned in prophecy appear for the last time in Revelation 20. Satan, who entered human history early in the Book of Genesis, here meets his doom. Earth and heaven pass away. Death and Hades, or Sheol, are banished forever.

This chapter speaks of two companies of people who are raised from the dead. What is called the first resurrection takes place when the Lord returns to the earth to establish his kingdom. Righteous persons will be raised from the dead to live and reign with Christ for a thousand years, but "the rest of the dead lived not until the thousand years were finished" (Rev. 20:5). The final resurrection, called by Christ "the resurrection of damnation" (John 5:29), will take place at the end of the millennial kingdom.

At that time death and Hades will deliver up the dead which were in them. Death, which has claimed the unsaved from the beginning of the human race, will finally surrender their bodies for the judgment of the great white throne. Hades will give up the souls and spirits which have been imprisoned there. Bodies, souls, and spirits will be reunited in this final resurrection of the unjust. The dead will stand before God.

This is not the record of a trial, but of a judgment. No one will be permitted to plead his case, because all the evidence needed will be contained in the books God has kept. The only destiny mentioned in this scene is the lake of fire. Salvation is not at issue: "it is the gift of God: not of works, lest any man should boast" (Eph. 2:8, 9).

One purpose of this great assize may be to determine degrees of punishment for the dead. It is revealed that some will receive "few stripes" and others "many stripes" (Luke 12:47). The ancient Sinai manuscript of the Bible renders this passage, "They were condemned every one, according to their deeds."

After the judgment, "Death and hell [Hades, lit.] were cast into the lake of fire" (Rev. 20:14). It is usually assumed that death and Hades are personalized in this statement; Revelation 6:8 is cited as an example: "Behold a pale horse: and his name that sat on him was Death, and Hell [Hades, lit.] followed with him." In this view, death and Hades are depicted as persons or entities, in a symbolic picture of their final banishment from the universe.

A literal view is simpler. In this passage "death" may refer to the bodies of all who have come up from the realm of death, and Hades may refer to the souls and spirits of those who have come up from that place during the last resurrection. With bodies, souls, and spirits reunited in the resurrection of damnation, the dead who have stood before the great white throne will be cast into the lake of fire. The meanings of "death" and "Hades" would then be equivalent to the statement found in Revelation 20:15: "Whosoever was not found written in the book of life. . . . "

One thing is for certain: in this passage Hades does not refer to the *place* which has given up its dead; that place will have vanished when heaven and earth flee away from the presence of the one who occupies the throne. A parallel use of language occurs in Jude 1:7, where "Sodom and Gomorrah, and the cities about them . . . [gave] themselves over to fornication." "Sodom and Gomorrah" obviously refers to the occupants of those cities, not to the places made up of houses and streets.

The final end of the unsaved is called the second death, the lake of fire. It means eternal separation from God. If this seems to be a far worse punishment than we think is warranted, it must be remembered that no one will go there except by his own choice. The wages of sin is death, and that includes the second death.

CHAPTER 12
THE OPENING OF
THE BOOKS OF GOD

It is perfectly reasonable that God should keep books. Even earthly businesses cannot be conducted apart from the keeping of books, and heaven conducts the affairs of the entire universe. Books are mentioned about 190 times in the Bible; for example, there are references to the book of the law, the book of the chronicles of the kings of Judah, the book in which our tears are recorded (Ps. 56:8), the sealed book of Daniel 12:4, the book of life.

The opening of books is associated with major turning points in God's dealings with the human race. Christ began his earthly ministry by opening the Bible. The judgments of God in the earth will be introduced by the opening of another book. When the great white throne brings the unsaved dead of all ages together before God, "the books" will be opened. Of special interest to the people of God will be the opening of the Lamb's book of life and the opening of the book of remembrance, where the good deeds of believers are inscribed.

When Jesus entered the synagogue at Nazareth he was given the book of the prophet Isaiah. He opened it and read the words, "The Spirit of the Lord is upon me, because he hath anointed me to preach the gospel to the poor; he hath sent me to heal the brokenhearted, to preach deliverance to the captives, and recovering of sight to the blind, to set at liberty them that are bruised, to preach the acceptable year of the Lord" (Luke 4:18, 19).

Upon opening that book Christ opened a new era in human

history, an era during which God will accept all who come to him in response to the invitation, "Come unto me, all ye that labour and are heavy laden, and I will give you rest" (Matt. 11:28). We are now living in the acceptable year of the Lord. We are "accepted in the beloved" because we have believed the gospel (Eph. 1:6).

The simple act of opening a book is fraught with deep meaning. It marks an epochal change in God's program for mankind, the dawn of the age of grace. It is also an example of the supreme importance of the written Word in the ministry of Christ, which began with this simple act. Christ's relationship to the Bible began with his birth, extended throughout his life, and continued after his death. The first mention of the Scriptures in connection with our Lord is found in a passage having to do with his birth—Hebrews 10:5, 7, 10: "When he cometh into the world" he said to God the Father, "[A] body hast thou prepared me. . . . Then said I, Lo, I come (in the volume of the book it is written of me) to do thy will, O God. . . . By the which will we are sanctified through the offering of the body of Jesus Christ once for all."

There can be no question as to when Jesus came into the world. It was when he was born in Bethlehem. As he lay there in the manger, he could have dismissed the universe with a word, for he was its Creator. Instead, he spoke with his Father about the body God had prepared for him. He knew he had come into the world to take that body to the cross and die to save a people destined to become his bride. The text he quoted—Psalm 40:6, 8—he knew by heart. He was its author.

Throughout his life Christ lived according to the Word. He preached the Word, overcame Satan by using the Word, and gave the Word to his disciples. And on his last day, as he hung on the cross, not even the agony of death could blot out the Word from his mind: there was one brief prophecy of Calvary still unfulfilled, a part of one sentence in Psalm 69:21: "In my thirst they gave me vinegar to drink." He had been offered vinegar earlier, "and when he had tasted thereof, he would not drink" (Matt. 27:34). But now the burning thirst of crucifixion had come upon him, and "Jesus knowing that all things were now accomplished, that the scripture might be fulfilled, saith, I thirst" (John 19:28). "When Jesus therefore had received the vinegar, he said, It is finished: and he bowed his head, and gave up the ghost" (19:30).

So precise is the fulfillment of prophecy that vinegar merely offered to Christ before he thirsted on the cross did not fulfill what was written. When he did thirst afterward, his cry "I thirst" did not mean he wanted someone to bring him water. It was "that the scripture might be fulfilled." The Word could not be broken. Christ could not surrender his spirit to the Father until every last detail written about his sufferings and death had taken place. Only after he received the vinegar was he able to say, "It is finished."

Much has been written about the three final words uttered from the cross. It has been recognized that our salvation became an accomplished fact when Christ said, "It is finished." But the primary meaning of the phrase is that the perfect fulfillment of the last brief prophecy was now finished.

After his resurrection Christ was walking with two disciples on the road to Emmaus. The written Word was still prominent in his ministry. "Beginning at Moses and all the prophets, he expounded unto them in all the scriptures the things concerning himself" (Luke 24:27; see 24:32). Earlier in the same chapter we read that the two beings in shining garments who appeared at the sepulchre expressed surprise that the Lord's followers did not remember the words Christ had spoken, or where he stood when he spoke them (24:5-7).

When Christ returns to the earth, the name he bears will emphasize again his identification with the Scriptures: "He was clothed with a vesture dipped in blood: and his name is called The Word of God" (Rev. 19:13). This has been one of his names from all eternity (John 1:1).

The Scriptures prophesy that Christ will again open a book on the day of vengeance. The last words Christ read from the Book of Isaiah were, "to preach the acceptable year of the Lord" (Luke 4:19). He did not read the words that followed, "and the day of vengeance of our God" (Isa. 61:2). The reason is perfectly clear. When he came to earth the first time, he had not come to deal in vengeance, but to bring salvation by his death. When the present age has run its course, however, the time will have come for divine wrath and vengeance. In John's vision of heaven, the Lamb is seen taking a book out of the Father's hand at that time. When he opens its seals, the four horsemen of the Apocalypse will ride forth into the earth. Men will experience war, famine, pestilence, martyrdom, earthquake, and the wrath of the Lamb (Rev. 5, 6).

After the seven final years of trouble for the human race, Christ will return with power and great glory, and sit on the throne of his glory. Before him will be gathered all nations (Matt. 25:31, 32). Daniel provides us with a clear description: "A fiery stream issued and came forth from before him: thousand thousands ministered unto him, and ten thousand times ten thousand stood before him: the judgment was set, and the books were opened" (Dan. 7:10).

The context makes it clear that "the books" are documents related to the judgment which follows the return of Christ to the earth, when dominion is taken away from the kings of the earth, and the beast is given to the burning flame. The nations gathered before the Lord will be separated into two groups on the basis of what is written in those books. One group will be invited to enter the kingdom prepared for them from the foundation of the world, the other will be sent to the everlasting fire prepared for the devil and his angels.

The best known reference to God's books is found in the description of the great white throne judgment (Rev. 20:11-15). This judgment will come after Christ's reign in the millennial kingdom, and it will take place far from earth. Heaven and earth will flee from the dread occupant of the throne. The unsaved dead of all the ages will stand before the Lord to be judged for the way they lived on earth.

These individuals are repeatedly called "the dead." Christians will already have been living in their resurrected bodies in the presence of the Lord for a thousand years. They will not be at this gathering, for the Lord has promised, "He that heareth my word, and believeth on him that sent me, hath everlasting life, and shall not come into condemnation; but is passed from death unto life" (John 5:24). There will be no pleading or argument. Perfect truth and justice will prevail.

It is the "book of life" (Rev. 20:15) which will determine the eternal fate of the human race. Revelation reveals a lot about this book. The book not only guarantees deliverance from the second death; it ensures that an individual will never be a worshipper of the Antichrist. Those who do worship him are people "whose names are not written in the book of life of the Lamb slain from the foundation of the world" (13:8).

Another revelation about the book of life is found in the statement concerning who will have a part in the holy city, the new Jerusalem, when it descends out of heaven from God: "There shall in no wise enter into it any thing that defileth, neither whatsoever worketh abomination, or maketh a lie: but they which are written in the Lamb's book of life" (Rev. 21:27). This means far more than deliverance from the lake of fire. It is a positive declaration of citizenship in the eternal city of God, the place the Lord went away to prepare for his followers (John 14:2).

So far as we can learn from Scripture, the book of life has never yet been opened. Even so, we are not left without clear teaching on how we may know our names are written there. One of the seven letters sent from heaven to earth by the ascended Lord contains this statement: "He that overcometh, the same shall be clothed in white raiment; and I will not blot out his name out of the book of life, but I will confess his name before my Father, and before his angels" (Rev. 3:5). Christ made the same promise while he was on the earth: "Whosoever therefore shall confess me before men, him will I confess also before my Father which is in heaven" (Matt. 10:32). The two groups Christ promises to confess before his Father are one and the same. Overcomers are people who have exercised faith in Jesus as the Son of God (1 John 5:4, 5). Those who confess him publicly as their resurrected Savior have the promise, "thou shalt be saved" (Rom. 10:9).

We can be as sure our names are in the book of life as Paul was about the inclusion of the names of Euodias and Syntyche, of whom he wrote, "[their] names are in the book of life" (Phil. 4:3). Our names will never be blotted out if we have trusted Christ, sealing our faith by acknowledging him in the presence of others. Many Christians assume our names are written in the book at the time we receive Christ as Savior, but it is more likely that they are put there before "the foundation of the world" (Rev. 17:8). This would suitably explain God's response when Moses asked to be blotted out of God's book: "Whosoever hath sinned against me, him will I blot out of my book" (Exod. 32:33).

Believers have long cherished the beautiful words of Malachi 3:16, 17: "Then they that feared the Lord spake often one to another; and the Lord hearkened, and heard it, and a book of remembrance was written before him for them that feared the Lord, and that thought upon his name. And they shall be mine, saith the Lord of hosts, in that day when I make up my jewels." This statement was written at a time when the church was not yet revealed to God's prophets, but believers today believe there is a book of remembrance kept for them also, because of the literal meaning of the Hebrew word translated "jewels." It means "a peculiar treasure," and it is so translated in Exodus 19:5. Christians are called "a people for his own possession" (Titus 2:14, lit.).

We have seen that books will be opened when the nations are judged, when the wicked dead stand before God at the great white throne, and when the Lord remembers the faithfulness of his Old Testament saints. Thus it is understandable that believers should speak of a recording angel (Eccles. 5:6), and that they should think of God's books when they think of receiving rewards at the judgment seat of Christ. Records would seem to be necessary as the basis for the granting of the crowns to faithful Christians some day. "Your labour is not in vain in the Lord" (1 Cor. 15:58).

The very hairs of our heads are numbered. Our most insignificant deeds are known to God. He will render to every man according to his deeds (Rom. 2:6-11). What we have done in the body will come up in remembrance before God (2 Cor. 5:10).

When the Lord sent out seventy obscure disciples to minister in his name, they returned later with joy saying, "Lord, even the devils are subject unto us through thy name" (Luke 10:17). He replied, "In this rejoice not, that the spirits are subject unto you; but rather rejoice, because your names are written in heaven" (Luke 10:20).

PART III
THE FUTURE OF THE CHURCH

CHAPTER 13
THE LAST DAYS
OF THE PRESENT AGE

Expressions like "the last days" and "the latter days" appear in the Bible over thirty times. Some of these passages are better known than others. The Bible's oldest book records Job's words, "I know that my redeemer liveth, and that he shall stand at the latter day upon the earth" (Job 19:25). As Jacob lay on his dying bed he called his twelve sons and said to them, "Gather yourselves together, that I may tell you that which shall befall you in the last days" (Gen. 49:1). God promised Moses that he would come to the aid of Israel in that time "when thou art in tribulation, and all these things are come upon thee, even in the latter days" (Deut. 4:30; see 4:27). Ezekiel predicted that Palestine would be invaded by a confederacy of nations from the north "in the latter days" (Ezek. 38:8). Daniel placed the rise of the king of fierce countenance, the Antichrist, in the same period (Dan. 8:23). One of Isaiah's best known prophecies describes the city of Jerusalem as the center of world government and worship in the last days (Isa. 2:2-4).

The period of time referred to in these and other Old Testament prophecies should not be confused with the last days of the church described in the New Testament. *Israel* and *the church* represent different parts of the divine program. The church does not appear in Old Testament prophecy; it will be gone from the earth before Israel's last days begin. Nevertheless, predictions about Israel and the nations are sometimes used in attempts to show that the end of the church age is near.

137

The point is made that since these prophecies will not be fulfilled until after the rapture has taken place, recent tendencies toward their fulfillment prove that the translation of the church is imminent.

Prominent among such Old Testament passages are those which make it clear that Israel is to be a nation in her own land again during her last days. It is evident, though, that no one can determine how much time will pass between the present situation in Israel and the return of Christ. It is often overlooked that the divine restoration of all Jews to the promised land will not take place until after the second coming of Christ (Deut. 30:1-3). What we observe in the Middle East today is not the divine restoration frequently announced in Scripture, but a preliminary return (in unbelief) of a portion of dispersed Israel. This is in keeping with what is written about conditions in the land when the latter days draw near.

Predictions about the Gentile nations are cited as further proof that the end may be near, and no one can deny the significance of world conditions in our own time. In the last days there will be a great military power to the north of Israel, capable of leading an invasion of the land (Ezek. 38, 39). To the south, African nations will awaken (Dan. 11:40). The people of the east will become powerful enough to send armies to fight in Armageddon (Rev. 16:12). In the west a confederacy of nations will be formed.

Scripture also contains references to general conditions existing on the earth in the latter times. Christ said "the days of the Son of man," that is, the time of his return to the earth, will be like the days of Noah and the days of Lot (Luke 17:26, 28). The earth was filled with violence when Noah lived, and perversion was prevalent during the time when Lot was a citizen of Sodom. Daniel wrote, "Many shall run to and fro, and knowledge shall be increased" (Dan. 12:4). Modern travel and the explosion of knowledge and communication have often been mentioned as a possible fulfillment of these words.

Christ warned of the coming of "distress of nations, with perplexity," and "men's hearts failing them for fear

[of] . . . those things which are coming on the earth" (Luke 21:24, 26). Evidently something is going to threaten the very existence of the human race: "except those days be shortened, there should no flesh be saved" (Matt. 24:22). As we have seen, an evil dictator will appear who will introduce a world government, a world religion, and a world economy. Recent tendencies toward world alliances, a world church, and the dependence of nations on each other in commerce and industry seem to point toward the early fulfillment of this prophecy (see Rev. 13).

There is nothing wrong with comparing world conditions to what is written in the Scriptures. One must take care, however, that such a comparison does not lead to speculation injurious to the study of the prophetic Word. In reality, it is not necessary to turn to Old Testament prophecy for light on the question of the imminence of the latter days. The New Testament contains many clear statements about conditions during the closing days of the church. This body of truth was given for our learning, on whom the ends of the ages have come (1 Cor. 10:11).

God wants his people to know when great events are impending. When he was about to destroy the cities of the plain, he said, "Shall I hide from Abraham that thing which I do . . . ?" Then he told Abraham of his plans (Gen. 18:17-22). It was revealed to Daniel that "the wise shall understand" in the time of the end (Dan. 12:10). When the Pharisees failed to comprehend the divine program in their day, Christ rebuked them with the words, "When it is evening, ye say, It will be fair weather: for the sky is red. And in the morning, It will be foul weather to day: for the sky is red and lowring. O ye hypocrites, ye can discern the face of the sky; but can ye not discern the signs of the times?" (Matt. 16:2, 3). Christians are admonished to exhort one another, "and so much the more, as ye see the day approaching" (Heb. 10:25). We do not go beyond what is written when we conclude that the end of the age may be near, on the basis of what the Scriptures say.

There are notable differences between prophecies dealing

with Christ's second coming and what has been revealed for the enlightenment of the church concerning its future. Important signs and time words have been given to the Jews; none are found in the church epistles. The simplest of terms are used with reference to the coming of the Lord for his church: "I will come again" (John 14:3); "the Lord himself shall descend from heaven" (1 Thess. 4:16); and "be patient . . . unto the coming of the Lord" (James 5:7).

In strong contrast, Israel has been told, "The sun shall be turned into darkness, and the moon into blood, before the great and the terrible day of the Lord come" (Joel 2:31); "When ye therefore shall see the abomination of desolation, spoken of by Daniel the prophet, stand in the holy place. . . . Then shall be great tribulation, such as was not since the beginning of the world to this time, no, nor ever shall be" (Matt. 24:15, 21); "Immediately after the tribulation of those days shall the sun be darkened, and the moon shall not give her light . . . and then shall appear the sign of the Son of man in heaven: and then shall all the tribes of the earth mourn, and they shall see the Son of man coming in the clouds of heaven with power and great glory" (Matt. 24:29, 30).

Believers today are not told to watch for the Jews to return to Palestine, for the rise of the Antichrist, for the beginning of the great tribulation, or for signs among the nations. Instead, they have been given information about their own age and what conditions will be like when the age approaches its close. None of the following passages by itself may be conclusive, but when all are taken together they become quite convincing. However, these passages cannot be considered the basis for setting the date at which Christians are to be taken away from the earth.

1. Perilous times will come.

This know also, that in the last days perilous times shall come. For men shall be lovers of their own selves, covetous, boasters, proud, blasphemers, disobedient to parents, unthankful, unholy, without natural affection, trucebreakers, false accusers, incontinent, fierce, despisers of those that are good, traitors, heady, highminded, lovers of pleasures more than lovers of God; having a form of godliness, but denying the power thereof: from such turn away. (2 Tim. 3:1-5)

The perilous times here described are different from the time of tribulation which will end the history of Israel. The difficult days predicted for the age of the church will be caused by wicked men, not by the wrath of God. There are different opinions about the identity of these evil men. Some think they are depraved men of the world; others understand them to be people within the corrupt church. Evidently they will be religious, because they will have "a form of godliness, but denying the power thereof." They will profess to be followers of God but will deny him in their actions (Titus 1:16).

There are nineteen instructive words and phrases in this passage, but they have received little attention in the Bible commentaries. Four things will be lacking in such individuals: obedience to parents, thankfulness, holiness, natural affection. Five times in the original text, some form of the word for "love" appears. These men will love themselves, they will love money and pleasure, but they will not love God or those who are good. The term "false accusers" is *diabolos* in the original. It means a slanderer, and is used as a title for Satan over thirty times (e.g., Rev. 12:9). The word translated "perilous" here is found in only one other place in the New Testament, where it describes a demon-possessed man (translated "fierce," Matt. 8:28).

These perilous times predicted for the last days of the church will be difficult for parents, because their children will increasingly be disobedient as natural affection is replaced by love of self. Such times will be difficult for good people in general because they will be despised by the unholy and fierce among whom they will be living. Difficult days will come to government when traitors increase (business and industry may well be included here, in view of the growing menace of industrial espionage). Pastors and missionaries will face hard days when the love of pleasure will have become more prevalent than the love of God, and when his power to save and transform men is denied.

2. There will be trouble between capital and labor.

> Go to now, ye rich men, weep and howl for your miseries that shall come upon you. . . . Ye have heaped treasure together for the last days. Behold, the hire of the labourers who have reaped down your fields, which is of you kept back by fraud, crieth: and the cries of them which have reaped are entered into the ears of the Lord of Sabaoth. (James 5:1, 3, 4)

Evidently, neither communism nor any other political system is going to succeed in redistributing the world's wealth. The rich will build up their estates until the very end. Their money will not prevent them from experiencing the miseries or calamities of the last days. The working class will continue to exist, along with capitalists and rich employers. Relations between capital and labor will be difficult.

The rich have defrauded the poor throughout history, and the centuries have witnessed many protests. The new emphasis in the situation described by James is that the cries of labor will be heard by the Lord. Of course, believers are primarily in view (James 5:7). This is significant because it will immediately precede the return of the Lord. "Be patient therefore, brethren, unto the coming of the Lord. . . . the coming of the Lord draweth nigh. . . . the judge standeth before the door" (5:7-9).

When the people of Israel in the days of Moses cried out to the Lord in their affliction, God heard their cry, and came down to deliver them (Exod. 3:7, 8). When working people cry out to him in great distress during the last days, their cries will reach his ears, and his coming will not be far away. He will be at the door.

3. False teachers will win a large following.

> But there were false prophets also among the people, even as there shall be false teachers among you, who privily shall bring in damnable heresies, even denying the Lord that bought them, and bring upon themselves swift destruction. And many shall follow their pernicious ways; by reason of whom the way of truth shall be evil spoken of. (2 Pet. 2:1, 2)

Peter is writing about the last days (2 Pet. 2:9; 3:3). Just as false prophets were prominent in the Old Testament, false teachers are mentioned during the church age. When they begin to win large numbers of followers, swift destruction will be imminent. The Lord's coming will be near.

The presence of false teachers is nothing new. They have been around ever since the church began. Paul warned of their coming and called them grievous wolves who would draw away many disciples (Acts 20:29, 30).

The multitudes claimed by leaders of false cults in recent years is a new phenomenon. There are millions of cult followers. Their presses run continuously, producing vast quantities of literature to be distributed worldwide. They gain publicity at the expense of the truth, complicating the work of true servants of the Lord. Their destructive heresies are blindly accepted by people who don't take the time to examine the Scriptures for themselves. If the presence of false teachers is not in itself an indication of the approaching end times, their success in winning a large following certainly is.

4. Bible prophecy will come under attack.

> Knowing this first, that there shall come in the last days scoffers, walking after their own lusts, and saying, Where

is the promise of his coming? for since the fathers fell asleep, all things continue as they were from the beginning of the creation. (2 Pet. 3:3, 4)

In this passage Peter does not seem to be speaking of atheists or agnostics. He is referring to people within the professing church—for they accept the Bible teaching about the creation. Yet they do not honor the precepts of Scripture. They are of bad moral character and they walk after their lusts. The object of their scoffing is not the ethical teachings of the Sermon on the Mount, but the promise of the second coming of Christ.

Peter's words could hardly have been fulfilled until after the beginning of the twentieth century. The doctrine of the return of the Lord had been forgotten by the church for hundreds of years. Most churchgoers were not aware of the many Scripture verses declaring Christ will come back again. Near the close of the nineteenth century the lost doctrine of the second coming was rediscovered simultaneously in various parts of the world. Students of the Word began to hold Bible conferences dealing with the theme. Prophetic sermons were preached everywhere and considerable literature was produced. With the rediscovery and proclamation of the good news of Christ's coming, enemies of the truth began to speak out against it. Peter's words then found fulfillment.

5. All nations will hear the gospel.

And they sung a new song, saying, Thou art worthy to take the book, and to open the seals thereof: for thou wast slain, and has redeemed us to God by thy blood out of every kindred, and tongue, and people, and nation; and hast made us unto our God kings and priests: and we shall reign on the earth. (Rev. 5:9, 10)

Here we see people from every nation in heaven. To be saved, these people will have had to hear and believe the gospel. Throughout most of the history of the church, however, large parts of the world were unevangelized. Thus, this passage means the gospel will be proclaimed in all nations before the Lord returns.

Only in recent decades has the message of the cross been carried to the uttermost parts of the earth. A new day dawned when gospel radio broadcasts began to reach people never before touched by the gospel. Hundreds of missionaries have penetrated the jungles to minister to unevangelized tribes. Uncounted millions of copies of Bibles, Testaments, and Scripture portions, in hundreds of languages, have been distributed in all corners of the earth.

Some Christians believe that Mark 13:10 refers to the church age: "And the gospel must first be published among all nations." Another passage which seems definitely to speak of the present age is Mark 4:26-29, which likens the kingdom of God to the sowing of seed. "When the fruit is brought forth, immediately he putteth in the sickle, because the harvest is come" (4:29). Parallel to this is Revelation 14:15: "Thrust in thy sickle, and reap: for the time is come for thee to reap; for the harvest of the earth is ripe." The harvesting is the time of divine judgment; this follows the gathering up of the fruit produced by the sowing of the seed of the Word (Luke 8:11), in the field of the world (Matt. 13:38).

6. There will be a great apostasy.

> Now the Spirit speaketh expressly, that in the latter times some shall depart from the faith, giving heed to seducing spirits, and doctrines of devils; speaking lies in hypocrisy; having their conscience seared with a hot iron. (1 Tim. 4:1, 2)

This departure from the faith is a deliberate rejection of divinely revealed truth. The same revelation is given elsewhere. "That day shall not come, except there come a falling away [apostasy, lit.] first" (2 Thess. 2:3). The present widespread rejection of the church's position regarding the deity of Christ, the inspiration of the Scriptures, and other fundamental doctrines may mean the final great apostasy has begun. In churches all over the world where the gospel was once preached faithfully, sermons are now devoted to subjects which have no foundation in the truth of God. Any teaching which denies or substitutes something else for the clear declarations of the Word, is likely to be what Paul calls a doctrine of demons.

Apostasy has always existed. What the Bible predicts for the last days is such a widespread turning away from the faith as to be worthy of being called "The Apostasy." To many, this sounds like a description of the days in which we live.

The concluding words in this passage are a strong reminder of the need for respecting prophetic Scriptures: "If thou put the brethren in remembrance of these things, thou shalt be a good minister of Jesus Christ, nourished up in the words of faith and of good doctrine, whereunto thou hast attained" (1 Tim. 4:6). "These things" are words of prophecy dealing with the last days of the church.

7. Christians will know the day is approaching.

> Exhorting one another: and so much the more as ye see the day approaching. (Heb. 10:25)

Christians who read the Bible with attention will know when world conditions become like those described as the last days. They will recognize the end times when they experience grievous times as evil men multiply, when wage earners cry to God because they find themselves in trouble, and when false teachers lead many astray. Believers will know the final day approaches as they see the doctrine of the second coming scoffed at, as the gospel reaches out into all the world, and as the apostasy deepens.

All of these revelations are unlike the signs which mark the coming of Christ at his second advent. The evidence that points to the imminence of the rapture is cumulative, developing over a period of time. No single mark of the last days is decisive, but when all of them appear together, we are justified in believing our generation may be the final one before the rapture.

We should be "looking for that blessed hope, and the glorious appearing of the great God and our Saviour Jesus Christ" (Titus 2:13). We can be waiting for God's Son from heaven (1 Thess. 1:10). It is the part of wisdom to watch and be sober (1 Thess. 5:6). We would be wise to exhort others as we see the day drawing near (Heb. 10:25). Most important, we can cleanse ourselves from all known sin: "Every man that hath this hope in him purifieth himself, even as he is pure" (1 John 3:3). If we do these things, we will be "found of him in peace, without spot, and blameless" (2 Pet. 3:14).

CHAPTER 14
KEPT FROM
THE TRIBULATION

The present world order will end with a display of divine wrath resulting in great tribulation for the human race. Hundreds of verses describe the terrors of this period. Destruction will come from the Almighty. In his fury God will send unprecedented distress and suffering to the inhabitants of the world. Multitudes will die. Men will hide in dens and rocks of the mountains for fear of the wrath of the Lamb. No such era has ever been known from the beginning of the creation, nor will such a period ever be seen again.

In spite of these appalling revelations, some Christians believe that the church will be present on earth during those years of unexampled tribulation. But there is no sound biblical basis for this view. A careful examination of all relevant passages of Scripture indicates that all believers will be taken to heaven before God unleashes his fury on the wicked of the world. Let us first consider a brief survey of the divine program of the ages, and where the church fits into it.

In the beginning the race was a single unit. There were no major divisions among the descendants of Adam and Eve except the growing segment of humanity that had become unrighteous. Sin became so prevalent that God began to unveil a plan for winning back his lost creation. He first called Abram out of the pagan city of Ur in Chaldaea. From the descendants of this one man God raised up a nation called Israel, through which he would give mankind his written Word and the Savior of the world. The race was now divided into Jews and Gentiles.

In New Testament days God introduced his present purpose of calling out from Jews and Gentiles a people for his name known as the church. Since the day of Pentecost there have been three major divisions of the race: The Jew, the Gentile, and the church of God (1 Cor. 10:32).

Four-fifths of the Bible deals primarily with the history of the Jews. In this account of Jewish history is a great deal of information about the Gentiles as well. One-fifth is given to the church of Jesus Christ—its origin, nature, doctrines, and destiny. Scattered throughout the Scriptures are references to the coming of a great tribulation in the latter days. Some remarkable and little recognized facts emerge from a study of these passages. First, such prophecies speak of the Jews and the Gentiles, but there are no predictions about a time of tribulation for the church. Second, when these latter days are described, Jews and Gentiles are found present on the earth, but the church is never mentioned. Third, reasons can be found why God will send a time of distress to both the Jews and the Gentiles, but there are no reasons why the final generation of Christians should be subjected to divine wrath.

The Bible contains many predictions about the tribulation that the Jews will face. Moses placed it in the last days (Deut. 4:27-30). Daniel described it as "a time of trouble, such as never was since there was a nation even to that same time: and at that time thy people [Israel] shall be delivered" (Dan. 12:1). Jeremiah called it "the time of Jacob's trouble" (Jer. 30:7). In the New Testament the people of Judaea are warned to flee to the mountains when they see the abomination of desolation standing in the holy place of their temple in Jerusalem, for that event marks the beginning of the great tribulation (Matt. 24:15-21). These Jewish people are counseled to "pray . . . [their] flight be not in the winter, neither on the sabbath day" (24:20), an example of how difficult it is to apply such passages to the church.

A time of tribulation is also predicted for the Gentiles. The Lord is going to "speak unto [the nations] in his wrath, and vex them in his sore displeasure" (Ps. 2:5). Every nation will drink the cup of the fury of God, "all the kingdoms of the world, which are upon the face of the earth" (Jer. 25:26; see also 25:15). This is God's "purpose that is purposed upon the whole earth: and this is the hand that is stretched out upon all the nations" (Isa. 14:26). No statements like these can be found about the church.

Hard and difficult times will come with the rise of evil men (2 Tim. 3:1-9), but those days have no resemblance to the tribulation which is to result from the pouring out of the wrath of God. Believers will experience chastening and affliction (Heb. 12:6). But the predicted period of distress is to be sent in wrath. It is not the chastening of a loving Father. When Christ warned his followers that tribulation awaited them in the world, he gave no indication that his words were intended only for the final generation who would be living at the time of his return (John 16:33). The tribulations of the hour are far different from the hour of tribulation.

It has often been observed that the church, after dominating the first three chapters of Revelation, disappears from view in chapters 4 through 18, which describe the day of vengeance. Most Christian commentators have concluded that the church is in heaven during that time. Near the end of the book the church reappears, associated with the Holy Spirit in heaven ("the Spirit and the bride say, Come," Rev. 22:17). The church, of course, is the bride of the Lamb (19:7; 21:9).

There are Old Testament analogies to the deliverance of the church before divine judgment is sent on the earth. For example, Noah was saved before the flood destroyed the ungodly, and righteous Lot was delivered before fire from heaven fell on the cities of the plain.

God tells us why the Jews and the Gentiles are to experience the tribulation, but no such information can be found about the church. Israel is to be refined and corrected; a remnant will be prepared for the part it must play in the earthly kingdom of Christ (Zech. 13:9). The Gentile nations are to be punished for their iniquity (Isa. 13:11), and a great multitude of people from all nations will be saved out of the tribulation to serve

God on earth during the kingdom when he dwells among men (Rev. 7:14, 15).

The destiny of the church, however, is heavenly. It needs no period of affliction to prepare it for an earthly kingdom. The church is a body of believers being called out from mankind over a period of nearly two thousand years. No one has been able to explain how the sufferings of Christians during the final seven years before the second coming of Christ could benefit them or the body of Christ. All Christians will be made perfect at the rapture. Why should the last generation need a time of tribulation to make them ready to join other believers at the translation of the entire church?

"God hath not appointed us to wrath, but to obtain salvation by our Lord Jesus Christ" (1 Thess. 5:9). The Son of God has "delivered us from the wrath to come" (1:10). "We shall be saved from wrath through him" (Rom. 5:9). The word "wrath" is applied in Scripture far more often to the time of tribulation than to eternal punishment. The prophets speak of it in this way (Isa. 13:9; Zeph. 1:18); the Book of Revelation so uses the term ten times (Rev. 16:1). Revelation also contains the promise of Christ to the church, "I will keep thee from the hour of temptation, which shall come upon all the world, to try them that dwell on the earth" (3:10). When that "hour" is mentioned next, the church does not appear in the text. Instead, we read of a company of Jews set apart as servants of God, and a multitude of Gentiles who are said to come out of the tribulation to serve the God who will dwell among them (Rev. 7; 21:3).

The nature of the church precludes its presence on the earth during the tribulation. The church is composed of a company of people altogether distinct from the Jews and the Gentiles, and it does not appear in the Old Testament. It is a part of the divine program God kept hidden from the prophets, so that nothing they wrote about the future can properly be applied to the church. It is a "mystery, which has kept secret since the world began, but now is made manifest" (Rom. 16:25, 26). The word "mystery" means a sacred secret previously withheld from men by God. The truth about the future existence of the church "from the beginning of the world hath been hid in God" (Eph. 3:9). Paul called it "the mystery which hath been hid from ages and from generations, but now is made manifest to his saints" (Col. 1:26).

Some have theorized that Israel and the church are identical. But the Word of God presents irreconcilable differences between the two. The Jews began with Abraham; the church began at Pentecost. The church was still to come when Christ said, "I will build my church" (Matt. 16:18). Israel is the subject of Old Testament prophecy; the church is not. The Jews worshipped at the temple in Jerusalem; the church worships wherever two or three are gathered in the name of Christ. The nation Israel is entered only by physical birth; the church by spiritual birth. Israel is one nation; the church is made up of individuals from every nation, including Israel. Israel's inheritance is the promised land; the church's inheritance is reserved in heaven. Israel was under law; the church is under grace.

The hope of the church has always been the imminent coming of Christ to call away his people to meet him in the air. Christians have looked for him to come at any moment, and have encouraged themselves in the fact that, according to prophecy, no event must take place before the rapture. They are admonished to be "looking for that blessed hope" (Titus 2:13), to wait for God's Son from heaven, and to purify themselves in view of his coming for them. The notion that Christians must pass through the tribulation does away with the imminency of Christ's promised return. It deprives believers of the greatest source of comfort to be found in Scripture. After the unconditional promise of the rapture in 1 Thessalonians 4:13-17, unmarred by any suggestion that anything must precede it, the Spirit concludes, "Wherefore comfort one another with these words" (4:18).

Many other passages support a pre-tribulation rapture. For example, there are no references to such a time in the New Testament descriptions of the last days, and each of these passages differs from what is written about the day of the Lord.

The tribulation is not mentioned in any of the church epistles. No reference to the rapture can be found in any description of the tribulation nor in any passage which speaks of the second coming of Christ to the earth. No instructions about living during the tribulation are given to the church.

Many Christians believe that the timing of John's call to heaven is significant. At the same time the church was mentioned for the last time, a door was opened in heaven and the apostle heard a voice say, "Come hither" (Rev. 21:9). Immediately he found himself in glory. This seems to be more than a coincidence, in view of the fact that what happened to Ezekiel, for example, portrayed coming events. It is certainly possible that John may be looked upon as representing the church at the rapture—he was called up at the exact moment the church disappears from the text.

Another fact to consider is that Scripture indicates there will be an interval between the rapture and Christ's second coming. This interval marks the rewarding of believers and the marriage of the Lamb. The opinion that the church will remain on the earth until Christ's second coming does not permit such an interval. Nor does it satisfactorily deal with the question of the destiny of people who are saved during the tribulation: will they belong to Israel or to the church?

During the years of tribulation, God will choose 144,000 people from all the tribes of Israel as his servants (Rev. 7:4). They will form the beginning of the remnant that God will call (Joel 2:32; Zeph. 3:13). It seems inconceivable that God should choose Israel for this ministry if the church still represents him on the earth. The clear implication of this revelation is that God will again be carrying on his purposes for the Jews after he has called his church away to heaven.

Furthermore, the Jews will be given special care by God at that time. Through Isaiah God warned them to hide "for a little moment, until the indignation be overpast" (Isa. 26:20). They have the promise that they will be saved out of the day of their trouble (Jer. 30:7). It was revealed to Daniel they are to be delivered (Dan. 12:1). Christ warned the people of

Judaea to flee to the mountains when the tribulation is about to begin (Matt. 24:16). When the devil is cast into the earth and seeks to destroy them, God will help them to fly into the wilderness to a place prepared for them, where they are fed for three and a half years (Rev. 12:6, 14). No such provision is made for the church; the best explanation for this is that it will not be present on earth then.

The people of Israel will become the objects of satanic persecution during the tribulation, but nothing is said of satanic persecution of the church. During the present age we are informed that our adversary, the devil, goes about seeking whom he may devour (1 Pet. 5:8). Christians are provided with weapons with which to quench his fiery darts (Eph. 6:16). We are to resist him and to stand against him. But there are no instructions given to the church about what to do to protect itself during those dreadful future years. This strange fact demands some explanation, for the presence of the devil on the earth will certainly be a matter of grave importance to the people of Israel.

When Christ gave his great Olivet Discourse—largely a prophecy of what lies ahead for the Jews—he said, "The gospel of the kingdom shall be preached in all the world for a witness unto all nations; and then shall the end come" (Matt. 24:14). That gospel was, "Repent ye: for the kingdom of heaven is at hand" (Matt. 3:2). It was preached by John the Baptist, by the apostles, and by Christ himself at his first appearing, when the kingdom was at hand in the person of its King. The gospel will be preached again prior to his second appearing—by his servants, the Jews. Then the kingdom will be established. This good news is a different message from the gospel of the grace of God preached today, which is, "Believe on the Lord Jesus Christ, and thou shalt be saved" (Acts 16:31). It will be preached until the fulness of the Gentiles has come in. Then Israel's blindness will be lifted (Rom. 11:25), and the good news entrusted to Israel will be proclaimed.

When the Lord returns to the earth at his second advent, "then shall all the tribes of the earth mourn" (Matt. 24:30).

These "tribes" are the tribes of Israel: the word is not used in any other sense in the New Testament. This is the fulfillment of Zechariah's prophecy, "They shall look upon me whom they have pierced, and they shall mourn for him, as one mourneth for his only son" (Zech. 12:10). It is consistent with other references to the sorrow with which the second coming of Christ will be received. "Behold, he cometh with clouds; and every eye shall see him, and they also which pierced him: and all kindreds of the earth shall wail because of him" (Rev. 1:7).

The rapture of the church, on the other hand, is an occasion for joy. Believers are told to "rejoice . . . that, when his glory shall be revealed, ye may be glad also with exceeding joy" (1 Pet. 4:13). They will be presented faultless before the presence of his glory with exceeding joy (Jude 1:24). It is difficult to attempt to reconcile the sorrow of Israel with the joy of Christians at the time of Christ's rapture of the saints. Thus these revelations evidently refer to different events.

All Scripture points to the fact that no unfulfilled prophecies lie between now and the imminent rapture. There will be no warnings or preparatory signs. The rapture will occur in the twinkling of an eye. We may rest assured that the Father will not pour out his divine wrath on the beloved bride of his Son.

CHAPTER 15
THE RAPTURE
OF THE CHURCH

Many people have good reason to fear coming events. But there are some who have no such fear. They are Christians who rejoice in the promise that believers will escape the dreadful things coming on the earth in the last days. They know that at any moment the rapture may snatch away all true followers of Christ from earth to heaven. Christians have anticipated this event ever since Christ announced it with the words, "I go to prepare a place for you. And if I go and prepare a place for you, I will come again, and receive you to myself; that where I am, there ye may be also" (John 14:2, 3).

For some twenty years after Christ made this promise, this was all anyone knew about the rapture. Then the Holy Spirit led Paul to write the letter we call First Thessalonians, and the revelation was greatly expanded.

One can imagine the excitement of the aged apostle John when that scroll first fell into his hands. The Lord had said long before, "I will come again." Just what had he meant by that? Through Paul the answer is given, "The Lord himself shall descend from heaven with a shout, with the voice of the archangel, and with the trump of God" (1 Thess. 4:16). What had the Lord meant when he said he would receive believers to himself? The Spirit declares, "The dead in Christ shall rise first: then we which are alive and remain shall be caught up together with them in the clouds, to meet the Lord in the air" (4:16, 17). Did the Lord intend to be understood literally when he said Christians will someday be where he is? Simply and briefly we are told, "and so shall we ever be with the Lord" (4:17). Not only shall we be with him; but we shall be with him forever!

These two passages, one by Christ and the other by Paul, form the heart of the New Testament teaching about how the present age will end. The next event prophesied in the Bible is the simultaneous withdrawal from the earth of every person who has accepted God's offer of salvation prior to that moment. A number of statements about this great event are to be found in various books of the New Testament, describing it in considerable detail.

The central passage in 1 Thessalonians 4:13-18 provides the basic outline of events. Christ, who ascended to heaven nearly two thousand years ago, will descend from heaven some day, as he promised. He will bring with him all who sleep in Jesus—the dead in Christ whose souls and spirits have been with him ever since their deaths. Their bodies will be resurrected and reunited with their souls and spirits. Then every believer who is still living at that time will be caught up together with them in clouds to meet the Lord in the air and to be with him forever.

Nothing like this revelation can be found in the Old Testament. It is a new prophecy, given only to the people of God who form the true church. It is altogether distinct from Old Testament prophetic themes dealing with the people of Israel and their land, the Gentile nations, and the created universe.

Christ's coming to take Christians to heaven is clearly distinguished in Scripture from his return to the earth to judge the world and to establish his kingdom. Christ will come to the *air* for the church; he will come to the *earth* at his second advent. He will come *for* his saints at the rapture; he will come *with* them afterward. The rapture is a New Testament revelation; the second coming is predicted in the Old Testament. All believers will be taken away for blessing when the Lord comes for his bride, the church; unbelievers will be taken away in judgment following his second coming. The rapture is im-minent, and no signs are given for it; the second coming will be preceded by a number of signs.

The Lord will call away Christians after he has completed his plan for taking from among all nations a people for his name (Acts 15:14). A specific, elect number of individuals will make up the completed church. It is written, "Blindness in part is happened to Israel, until the fulness of the Gentiles be come in" (Rom. 11:25). The fulness of the Gentiles is generally understood to mean the full number of Gentile believers who, with all saved Jews, will make up the body of Christ. It is a number known only to God. When the last individual of this number has received Christ, the rapture will take place.

The best way to comprehend the New Testament teaching regarding the rapture is to relate every passage to the outline of events given in 1 Thessalonians 4:16, 17. All revelations given elsewhere dovetail beautifully with the central teaching about the succession of these events.

1. The Lord will descend from heaven to the air above us.

Elsewhere it is said he will "come," he will "appear," and he will "return," but only in 1 Thessalonians do we read that "the Lord himself shall descend from heaven." Christ will leave his dwelling place, descend toward earth, stop somewhere in the air, and call every believer away to be with him forever. The same word translated "descend" appears in the original language of John 3:13, where it is revealed that Christ "came down from heaven" to win for himself a bride.

When he descends he will bring with him "them also which sleep in Jesus" (1 Thess. 4:14). The same truth is found in the previous chapter, where we read about "the coming of our Lord Jesus Christ with all his saints" (3:13). Believers have long been waiting for God's Son to return from heaven (1:10). As they have fallen asleep, one by one, over the centuries, their souls and spirits have ascended to glory where they live in his presence. The popular phrase that "we go to heaven when we die" does not appear in Scripture, but it is the clear teaching of the Word. To be absent from the body means to be present with the Lord (2 Cor. 5:8). To depart this life is to be with Christ (Phil. 1:23). When he descends from heaven, departed believers will accompany him to participate in the resurrection of the just.

He will come with a shout, with the voice of the archangel, and with the trump of God. Nothing is revealed as to whether these sounds will be heard by everyone or only by the people of God. The shout is a cry of command. It will be uttered by the Lord himself. The voice of the archangel will be the voice of Michael—he is the only archangel to be named in the Bible. The trump of God is "the last trump" of 1 Corinthians 15:52, to be sounded when the dead are raised and the living are changed. It is not to be confused with the seventh trumpet of Revelation 11:15, sounded by an angel during the tribulation long after the church has been called away.

2. The dead in Christ will rise.

When the Lord descends from heaven, the first event to take place on earth will be the resurrection of "the dead in Christ," called elsewhere "the out-resurrection from among the dead" (Phil. 3:11, lit.). When these "sleeping" believers rise, the bodies of all other deceased human beings will remain in their graves until the time for their resurrection has come.

Not all Christians agree that this resurrection will be limited to the church. Some think Old Testament believers will be included, but they face the problem that the expression "in Christ" is never found in the Old Testament, although it appears about sixty times in the New. To be in Christ is to be a member of his body, the church: "We are one body in Christ" (Rom. 12:5). It would be incongruous to apply these words to David, for example, who died a thousand years before the incarnation. The saints of other ages owe their salvation to what Christ did on Calvary, but they are unlike church saints in other respects. They differ in the place they occupy in God's unfolding plan, in the time of their resurrection, and in their destiny.

Furthermore, the resurrection which accompanies the rapture is called a mystery. It is a sacred secret never before revealed (1 Cor. 15:51, 52). God hid this truth from men throughout the centuries which preceded the New Testament revelation. Before the church came into existence people knew nothing of it.

The doctrine of resurrection itself was no mystery, of course. It was revealed to Daniel that the people of Israel would be raised from the dead after the tribulation (Dan. 12:1-3), and Job understood that his own resurrection would take place in the last days when the Redeemer would walk the earth (Job 19:25-27). In the New Testament, three resurrections are distinguished from each other by what follows each one as they take place in their own order (1 Cor. 15:23). When church saints are raised at the rapture, they will go to be with the Lord where they will receive the heavenly inheritance reserved for them (1 Pet. 1:4). The saints who are raised at the beginning of Christ's kingdom will live and reign with him for a thousand years (Rev. 20:4), while "the rest of the dead" (20:5) are later raised to stand before the great white throne of judgment.

Many have wondered whether children of Christian parents, and babies not yet born to expectant mothers, will participate in the rapture. Most theologians believe the grace of God will include them, even though there is no specific revelation about it. The children of believers occupy a place of special privilege. They are "holy" or separated to God by the belief of even one parent (1 Cor. 7:14). Children of unsaved parents will be raptured only if they are believers.

Bereaved parents are interested in knowing whether there will be babies in heaven. God will certainly not deprive anyone of anything needed for perfect happiness there; the following revelation may shed some light on this question: "When he shall appear, we shall be like him" (1 John 3:2). Christ was in the prime of his manhood when he was crucified at age thirty-three. If old people are to be like him at the rapture, presumably children will be also. It is written that we shall be satisfied, when we awake, with his likeness (Ps. 17:15). We shall all be faultless and perfect when that happens (Jude 1:24).

3. All believers will be caught up to meet the Lord in the air.

It is important to notice what is implied in the words "caught up together with them" (1 Thess. 4:17). Before the entire church is translated to meet the Lord, living believers will be reunited with those who fell asleep in Christ. The sequence, then, is resurrection, reunion, rapture.

Some details not found in 1 Thessalonians 4 are developed in other passages. For example, what will happen to the bodies of saints to prepare them for being caught up to heaven? In the twinkling of an eye, "the dead shall be raised incorruptible, and we shall be changed" (1 Cor. 15:52).

Our new bodies will be made incapable of ruin and decay. They will be glorious rather than dishonored and lacking in dignity, and powerful rather than weak. They will be designed for the life of the spirit (the spirit of man is that part of his immaterial being by which he is able to communicate with God). Our new bodies will be heavenly, not earthly. They will be immortal. Since we are to be like our risen Lord, we shall be as free as he was from the limitations imposed on humans by natural law.

How can such a tremendous change be brought about in the twinkling of an eye? The answer lies in a brief, hard-to-understand revelation: The Lord will "change our vile body, that it may be fashioned like unto his glorious body, according to the working whereby he is able even to subdue all things unto himself" (Phil. 3:21). The same divine energy that holds the universe together will change us at the rapture. Christ "uphold[s] all things by the word of his power" (Heb. 1:3).

Will Christians recognize their loved ones after they meet the Lord? Evidently they will. There is nothing in Scripture to suggest otherwise. The disciples recognized Moses and Elijah (whom they had never seen) at the transfiguration of Christ. The rich man knew who Abraham was when he saw the patriarch after death. We shall know at that time even as we are known today (1 Cor. 13:12). There is a reason why we are to be caught up together with those who have died in

Christ. We surely will not be among total strangers when the Lord calls us away.

The Scriptures contain no information about whether the rapture will be witnessed by the entire world. Christ's ascension was seen only by his followers. We know that when the Lord returns to the earth, "every eye shall see him" (Rev. 1:7), but no similar statement is to be found in descriptions of the rapture. The world may learn about it only when Christians are found to be missing. The rapture will certainly disrupt the kingdom of Satan. The devil is the prince of the power of the air; the Lord has chosen to meet his saints in the very realm of Satan, as though to demonstrate Christ's complete mastery over the kingdom of darkness.

4. We shall afterward be with the Lord forever.

The outline of events taking place at the time of the rapture concludes with the words, "and so shall we ever be with the Lord." There are several parallel statements elsewhere. Christ said he was coming to receive us to himself, "that where I am, there ye may be also" (John 14:3). He prayed, "Father, I will that they also, whom thou hast given me, be with me where I am, that they may behold my glory" (John 17:24). Paul wrote about "our gathering together unto him" (2 Thess. 2:1). Being with him forever includes ascending with him to heaven at the rapture, returning with him when he delivers his people Israel and brings Armageddon to an end, and sitting with him on the throne to reign over the universe forever.

One of the first things to happen to believers after they meet the Lord in the air will be the presentation of rewards for the way they lived on earth. We must all appear at the judgment seat of Christ (2 Cor. 5:10). This "judgment seat" carries no thought of condemnation. The term is translated from *bema*, the raised seat from which awards were given to those who won athletic contests.

After believers have received their rewards, the Holy Spirit will present the church to the Lord at the marriage of the Lamb: "He which raised up the Lord Jesus shall raise up us

163

also by Jesus, and shall present us with you" (2 Cor. 4:14). The Spirit who now keeps us from falling will present us faultless before the presence of his glory with exceeding joy (Jude 1:24).

CHAPTER 16
THE ORDER
OF THE RESURRECTIONS

What the Bible teaches about the resurrection of the human body is so widely misunderstood that it demands a separate treatment in any study of Bible prophecy. Many commentaries contain references to a "general resurrection," a term not found anywhere in Scripture. Christians who hear of this cannot be blamed for thinking it means the world will some day be overwhelmed by the sudden appearance of vast multitudes of resurrected people.

At the opposite extreme is the denial of a physical resurrection, a belief held by the Sadducees in Jesus' time (Matt. 22:23). This position is taken today by those who spiritualize certain Bible teachings. But if there is no resurrection, then the promises which have given hope to countless believers for centuries are not true, and "we are of all men most miserable" (1 Cor. 15:19).

When all of the Bible revelation on the subject is examined carefully, it becomes clear that all men will not be raised simultaneously. It will be "every man in his own order" (1 Cor. 15:23). The dead will be raised on three different occasions. They can be distinguished by observing what is written about the subjects of each resurrection, the time when each resurrection takes place, and what happens to those who are resurrected. The three occasions are (1) the resurrection of the dead in Christ at the rapture of the church, (2) the resurrection of Old Testament and tribulation saints at the second coming of Christ, and (3) the resurrection of "the rest of the dead" at the end of Christ's thousand-year reign over the earth.

The resurrection of believers from the present age should not be confused with that of believers from any other age. Paul referred to it as a mystery, a previously unrevealed part of God's program of the ages: "Behold, I shew you a mystery; We shall not all sleep, but we shall all be changed . . . and the dead shall be raised incorruptible" (1 Cor. 15:51, 52). The plan of God cannot be understood apart from the realization that nothing about the church was ever made known to God's people in ancient times (Col. 1:25-27). The raising of Christians from the dead at the time of the rapture is a part of this previously unrevealed body of truth. It is called "the out-resurrection from among the dead" (Phil. 3:11, lit.), a term found nowhere else. God will raise a particular company of believers, the dead in Christ, out from among the dead of the ages, so they may participate in the removal of the church from the earth to become the bride of Christ.

When Christ descends from heaven he will bring with him the souls and spirits of those who sleep in Jesus. Then the bodies of the dead in Christ will rise and be reunited with their souls and spirits in resurrection (1 Thess. 4:14, 16).

When does this scene take place? It follows the descent of Christ from heaven to the air to "snatch away" the church. It takes place before the tribulation, and at least seven years before the second coming of Christ to the earth.

What happens to those who take part in this resurrection of Christians? First, they are united with living believers, then they are taken away from the earth to meet the Lord in the air. Nothing like this was ever predicted for the people of God who lived in Old Testament times. It marks the beginning of the destiny of one company of believers (the church) which is quite different from what has been prophesied for saved Jews and Gentiles from previous ages.

The second company of people to be raised from the dead will be those believers who are still in their graves at the second coming of Christ to the earth. They include saved Jews and Gentiles from Old Testament times, together with the martyrs of the tribulation period, "beheaded for the witness of Jesus, and for the word of God (Rev. 20:4). Daniel spoke of them when he wrote, "Many of them that sleep in the dust of the earth shall awake, some to everlasting life" (Dan. 12:2). His language, while certainly including godly Jews, is flexible enough to include saved Gentiles as well. This is a primary reference to the future resurrection of Old Testament saints, although there are several others.

When does this scene take place? Daniel places it after the great tribulation, to which he refers in Daniel 12:1. The Book of Revelation likewise puts it after the tribulation, and after the second coming of Christ. The church will already have been taken from the earth some years before. Isaiah also links the resurrection of the Jews with "the indignation," a synonym for the tribulation (see Isa. 26:19-21). There can be no question of this chronology. The second coming of Christ is placed by Matthew "immediately after the tribulation of those days" (Matt. 24:29).

What happens to this resurrected company? Revelation 20:4 says they will live and reign with Christ a thousand years. Their reign is associated with the beloved city of Jerusalem, capital of the world during the kingdom (20:9). This is an earthly destiny. It should not be confused with the heavenly destiny of the resurrected church saints.

The third company of people to be resurrected is described in Revelation 20:5: "The rest of the dead lived not again until the thousand years were finished." The "rest of the dead" are the unsaved people of all the ages. Daniel also wrote of them: "Many from among those who sleep in the dust of the earth shall awake, these to everlasting life, but those (the rest of the sleepers, who do not awake at this time), shall awake to shame and everlasting contempt" (Dan. 12:2, lit. The material in parentheses is an interpolation by Jewish scholars.).

There are two resurrections in this passage with no indication of how long a time would elapse between them. In Christ's reference to "the resurrection of life" and "the resurrection of damnation" (John 5:29), no light is shed on the length of this interval. Paul spoke of "a resurrection of the dead, both of the just and unjust" (Acts 24:15), without saying anything about how far apart they would be. The length of the interval is not revealed until Revelation informs us it will be one thousand years.

What happens to this third company of the resurrected? They stand before the occupant of the great white throne to be judged, then they are cast into the lake of fire (Rev. 20:11-15).

The doctrine of the resurrection of the human body is no puzzle to anyone who compares these three groups of people. The entire human race will rise from the dead, but Scripture makes it clear they will not all be raised at the same time. Three distinct companies will be resurrected, each one in its own order.

CHAPTER 17
THE DESTINY
OF BELIEVERS

The Bible reveals what the destiny of believers will be: "Eye hath not seen, nor ear heard, neither have entered into the heart of man, the things which God hath prepared for them that love him. But God hath revealed them unto us by his Spirit" (1 Cor. 2:9, 10).

The first sentence of this passage is sometimes quoted as proof that we can know nothing about what lies ahead. The concluding sentence, however, affirms the exact opposite of this. The Bible contains a great deal of information about what happens after a Christian dies. It also tells us about what will happen to believers who will still be living when the present age comes to an end.

When a believer dies, he "falls asleep in Christ" (a New Testament euphemism for death). But only the body falls asleep. This expression is never used to refer to the death of the soul or the spirit.

The language of Scripture is restrained when it speaks of the death of God's people, which is far different from the death of unsaved people. When the body of a believer falls asleep, his soul and spirit go immediately to heaven: to be absent from the body is to be present with the Lord (2 Cor. 5:8). The same moment a Christian closes his eyes in death he opens them to behold the Lord in the glory of heaven. Every believer who ever lived and is now dead is consciously in the presence of the Lord.

No revelation has been given as to whether Christians in

heaven are aware of what is happening on earth, but there is an intimation that they do not. God says, "Behold, I create new heavens and a new earth: and the former shall not be remembered, nor come into mind" (Isa. 65:17). Surely the God who remembers our sins and iniquities no more (Heb. 8:12) will not let the joy of heaven be marred by the knowledge of the heartaches of loved ones nor by the memory of our own sins and failures while we lived on earth.

The Book of Psalms has always been a source of comfort and instruction to the sorrowing and the dying. One verse in particular has meant a great deal to those who are faced with the death of a loved one: "Yea, though I walk through the valley of the shadow of death, I will fear no evil: for thou art with me; thy rod and thy staff they comfort me" (Ps. 23:4). God's people face only the shadow of death, not death itself as unbelievers experience it. They simply walk through the dark valley, and the Lord is present with them constantly.

Falling asleep in Christ is the beginning of a new life. A friend of mine who had lost his little girl knows this well. When asked how many children he had, he said, "I have one in the land of the living and two still with me here in the land of the dying." Sorrow is much more bearable if we learn from God's Word what happens when a loved one dies. We know where our loved ones are, and that their present state is far better than the best we might have wished for them on earth. We know they are experiencing unutterable joy in the presence of the Lord (Ps. 16:1). For us who are left behind, heaven becomes nearer and dearer than it was before. We know that their separation from us is only temporary. Any day or night may bring them back to us when the Lord comes to take every Christian to himself at the translation of the church to heaven.

The greatest source of comfort in all the Bible for those who have had loved ones taken from them is found in the prophetic Word. The Lord will descend from heaven some day. In that moment all who died in Christ will rise from the dead. Then we who are alive and remain on earth will be caught up together with them to meet the Lord in the air, to be with him forever. This is the plain teaching of 1 Thessalonians 4:13-18. The passage concludes: "Wherefore comfort one another with these words."

If we should be among those believers who are living when the Lord descends from heaven to take his church away, we know what to expect. He will bring with him the souls and spirits of "the dead in Christ" who will have been with him in glory from the moment their bodies fell asleep. This is what is called "the coming of our Lord Jesus Christ with all his saints" (1 Thess. 3:13). Their bodies will be raised from the dead and changed to become like his own glorious body. They will be changed by that power which enables him to subdue all things unto himself (Phil. 3:21). In the twinkling of an eye all living believers will also be changed and made like him (1 Cor. 15:51-53). Then the entire company will be caught up to meet the Lord in the air, to be with him forever afterward (1 Thess. 4:17).

A lengthy description of these new bodies appears in 1 Corinthians 15:35-54. No two will be alike, so that the infinite variety we see on earth will be preserved. They will be celestial, or heavenly, rather than terrestrial. Decay and ruin will be things of the past, for these eternal bodies will be incorruptible. They will be glorious: Daniel spoke of them when he said some will shine as the brightness of the firmament, and as the stars (Dan. 12:3).

Because they will be raised in power, human weakness and frustration will be gone forever. The new bodies of Christians are described as spiritual—they will be keyed to the life of the spirit in an altogether new and different environment. Christians are also destined to become immortal, or no longer subject to death.

Wonderful as this extended description is, a brief statement in 1 John 3:2 surpasses it: "When he shall appear, we shall be like him." We are destined to become just as our Lord was after his resurrection. Events taking place on the day of his resurrection cast light on what this means.

When the disciples visited the empty tomb they noticed

something remarkable about the linen clothes in which the body of the Lord had been placed. The napkin—the cloth which had been wrapped around his head—is specifically mentioned. It was "not lying with the linen clothes, but wrapped together in a place by itself" (John 20:7). The expression "wrapped together" means literally "rolled up." The picture given is that of undisturbed grave clothes. The linens were still wrapped together in the same way they had been when he was buried. They still bore the impress of the body of Jesus, but he was gone. He had passed through the linen wrappings without disturbing them. It was this astonishing sight which caused them to know Christ had indeed risen from the dead.

As the eleven disciples were gathered together that same evening, the Lord suddenly stood among them, even though the doors were closed (John 20:19). He was able to move freely from one place to another, even ascending to heaven and returning at will.

Since all believers are to be like Christ after he takes them home to heaven, they too will no longer be subject to the natural laws which limit us now. It will be possible to pass through solid matter and to move about the universe in a way which would now be considered miraculous. This revelation is perfectly in keeping with what is written elsewhere about the heavenly bodies of Christians.

During the interval between the rapture of the church and the second coming of Christ to the earth, "We must all appear before the judgment seat of Christ; that every one may receive the things done in his body, according to that he hath done, whether it be good or bad" (2 Cor. 5:10). Every Christian will be included in this divine review. We will be given rewards based on the way we have lived on earth and the service we have rendered for the Lord. This judgment does not determine who shall enter heaven. That has already been decided on earth by an individual's response to the gospel message. Only Christians stand before this throne. Their sins are not reviewed. These were cancelled at the cross, to be "remember[ed] no more" (Heb. 10:17). Believers have the promise of Christ that they will never come into judgment with regard to everlasting life. They have already passed from death to life (John 5:24).

A detailed description of what takes place at the judgment seat of Christ is found in 1 Corinthians 3:9-15. Our deeds will be tested by fire. If they abide the test, we shall receive a reward. If our deeds are burned, we shall suffer the loss of rewards, but we ourselves shall be saved, "yet so as by fire" (3:15). The fire will not touch us, it is only our deeds that are tried. Our salvation will not be affected. Even the least worthy Christian will receive something from the Lord in that day: "Then shall every man have praise of God" (1 Cor. 4:5). Even a cup of cold water given to a thirsty soul because the giver is a disciple of Christ is to be rewarded (Matt. 10:42).

Human language is inadequate to describe the nature of our rewards, but we do know what we will be honored for. An incorruptible crown will be given to all who have kept the precepts of the Word of God (1 Cor. 9:25). A crown of rejoicing awaits those who have engaged in missionary work and soul winning (1 Thess. 2:19). A crown of righteousness is to be presented to all who have kept the faith and who have loved the appearing of Christ (2 Tim. 4:8). A crown of life will be given to those who have endured trials because they belong to the Lord (James 1:12). A crown of glory will reward believers who have fed the flock or who have been an example to others (1 Pet. 5:2-4).

The Bible makes it unmistakably clear the basis for rewards is faithfulness in the fulfillment of God's will. "Well done, thou good and faithful servant: thou hast been faithful over a few things, I will make thee ruler over many things: enter thou into the joy of thy lord" (Matt. 25:21). "Because thou hast been faithful in a very little, have thou authority over ten cities" (Luke 19:17). The most obscure Christian may receive as great a reward for faithful service as the most outstanding servant of the Lord. The five crowns are available to all believers, not just to a chosen few. God is no respecter of persons.

The marriage of the Lamb will follow the rewarding of the people of God (Rev. 19:7-9). The church will be united with

Christ (2 Cor. 11:2). Christ will present it to himself as his bride, a glorious church, without spot, wrinkle, or any other blemish (Eph. 5:27). The bride will be clothed in fine white linen, which is the righteousnesses, or good deeds, of the saints.

The marriage supper will take place after the wedding. We are not told where this is to be, but it is assumed it will be on the earth. Earthly saints are admonished to "wait for their lord, when he will return from the wedding" (Luke 12:36). In the parable of the ten virgins, some ancient manuscripts describe the virgins as waiting for "the bridegroom and the bride" (Matt. 25:1). This may be interpreted as an earthly scene, having to do with the kingdom of heaven, or with heaven's rule over the earth.

During the period when Christians are in heaven with their Lord, the tribulation will be taking place on earth. At its conclusion Christ will leave heaven with his bride and return to the earth to judge the nations and to establish his millennial kingdom. Second Thessalonians 1:10 refers to this event: "When he shall come to be glorified in his saints, and to be admired in all them that believe." Christ's saints are the raptured and rewarded individuals who form the universal church. Their transformation will be so remarkable that Christ, the Prince of glory, will actually be glorified in them. Those on earth who witness his return with his bride will admire the Lord and glorify him because of what he will have done for people who once were ordinary mortals, but who have now been made like their glorious Lord.

What lies ahead for Christians in eternity? For one thing, *there is knowledge to be gained*. The Bible tells us that when we see Christ, we shall know as we are now known (1 Cor. 13:12). Christ clarified this when he said, "This is life eternal, that they might know thee the only true God, and Jesus Christ, whom thou hast sent" (John 17:3). The human mind draws back in awe and wonder at what this means. We may feel limited now, or deprived of educational and other advantages, but some day we shall know God! He is the Creator who has never permitted two sunsets to be alike. He has never created two snowflakes which are identical. No two blades of grass, no two leaves are duplicates. All these things are expressions of the mind of God, yet eternal life will mean knowing him and partaking in some measure of his limitless knowledge.

Not only is there knowledge to be gained as our future unfolds, *there is work to do*. A remarkably concise phrase declares, "His servants shall serve him" (Rev. 22:3). What kind of service will we perform? Scripture gives us a picture of what some of our responsibilities will include: "Do ye not know that the saints shall judge the world? . . . Know ye not that we shall judge angels?" (1 Cor. 6:2, 3). This can only mean Christians will sit with Christ on the throne of his glory after he returns to the earth to judge the nations, or Gentiles (Matt. 25:31-46).

We will have a part with the Lord as he separates the Gentiles into two groups, sending one company into eternal doom and inviting the other company to enter the kingdom prepared for them. It is also revealed that sinning angels are now reserved in darkness awaiting the judgment of the great day (Jude 1:6). Believers will be associated with their Lord in that judgment.

A brighter side to the kind of work awaiting us has to do with every believer's inheritance (1 Pet. 1:3, 4). We are all heirs of God and joint heirs with Christ. Administering that inheritance may be a part of the way we shall serve him.

In eternity *we will have a destiny to fulfill* by reigning with Christ over the universe: "We shall reign on the earth" (Rev. 5:10); "[We] shall reign for ever and ever" (Rev. 22:5). The entire creation seems to be in view in the words of Isaiah: "Of the increase of his government and peace there shall be no end" (Isa. 9:7). We have this promise from the Lord: "To him that overcometh will I grant to sit with me in my throne, even as I also overcame, and am set down with my Father in his throne" (Rev. 3:21). These "overcomers" are not individuals who are more deeply spiritual than others, but simply those who have been born of God by believing on Christ (1 John 5:4, 5).

There is a mysterious connection between our future destiny of reigning with Christ and our present sufferings on earth:

"If we suffer, we shall also reign with him" (2 Tim. 2:12); "I reckon that the sufferings of this present time are not worthy to be compared with the glory which shall be revealed in us" (Rom. 8:18); "Our light affliction, which is but for a moment, worketh for us a far more exceeding and eternal weight of glory" (2 Cor. 4:17). Of all the Scripture passages on why Christians suffer pain, sickness, loneliness, and other afflictions, this is one of the most important. Our present sufferings point toward eternity.

An old Puritan pastor expressed it well when he said to his congregation one Sunday morning, "As the angels of God pass through our church today, they do not look on us as we may view ourselves—obscure, poor, and disadvantaged. Instead, they see us as God looks upon us, as though we were already clothed in the royal purple of universal sovereignty. They know God is now taking out from mankind a people for his name, that he is preparing us each one for that glorious destiny when we shall rule with the King of kings over his limitless creation." Such revelations should cause us to keep our eyes fixed on glory, to be willing to let God prepare us for a final destiny beyond imagination.

CHAPTER 18
HEAVEN

Somewhere in the universe is the dwelling place of God—heaven. The word "heaven" occurs more than seven hundred times in the Scriptures. In all but three of these verses it is translated from the Hebrew *shemayim*, the equivalent Chaldee word *shemayin*, or the parallel Greek *ouranos*. Literally these words mean "that which is above." The word is used in three different ways. It is used to mean the atmospheric heavens where clouds form (Matt. 24:30), winds blow (Ps. 78:26), and birds fly (Jer. 4:25). A second use is of the heavens of the stars and planets (Isa. 13:10; Ps. 19:1). The third distinct usage refers to the dwelling place of God (e.g., "your Father which is in heaven," Matt. 5:45).

The latter "heaven" is where Christ went at his ascension (Acts 1:11). From there he will return some day (1 Thess. 4:16). Because the apostle Paul called it "the third heaven" (2 Cor. 12:2), it is customary to speak of the atmospheric heavens as the first heaven and the starry skies as the second heaven. The word usually occurs in the plural form, as in Genesis 1:1, where God is said to have created the "heavens."

Many of the popular ideas about heaven have no basis in the Word of God. Peter is often depicted as standing at its gate screening all who seek to enter. This notion is doubtless based on Christ's words to Peter, "I will give unto thee the keys of the kingdom of heaven" (Matt. 16:19). The "kingdom of heaven," however, is God's rule over the earth, not his celestial abode.

The widely held belief that heaven is a city of streets lined with the mansions of Christians is not actually taught in Scripture. Christ said, "In my Father's house are many mansions," (John 14:2), but "mansions" here is more accurately rendered, "dwelling places." Heaven and earth were two of the dwelling places in the Father's great house at the time the Lord spoke these words. He said he was going away to prepare a place for his followers, not to build heavenly mansions for them. That place is believed to be the heavenly Jerusalem described in Revelation 21.

The Bible reveals a number of facts about the future home of the redeemed. Heaven is a real place, not a state of mind or a vague religious concept. From that place Christ came; to that place he returned after his resurrection. The day will come when "the Lord himself shall descend from heaven with a shout, with the voice of the archangel, and with the trump of God" (1 Thess. 4:16). The apostles were given this promise at his ascension: "This same Jesus, which is taken up from you into heaven, shall so come in like manner as ye have seen him go into heaven" (Acts 1:11).

In Scripture heaven is always said to be up. Christ was "taken up" while the disciples looked on, just as Elijah the prophet "went up by a whirlwind into heaven" in the sight of Elisha (2 Kings 2:11). On the island of Patmos the apostle John saw a door open in heaven, heard a voice cry, "Come up hither" (Rev. 4:1, 2). Believers know their destiny will bring them eventually to that place "high above the earth" (Ps. 103:11) where Christ went when he "ascended up on high . . . far above all heavens" (Eph. 4:8, 10), called "the heaven of heavens" by Moses (Deut. 10:14) and Solomon (1 Kings 8:27).

It has been suggested that heaven may be in the northern part of the sky, because of the implications of certain passages of Scripture. Ezekiel's heavenly vision came like a whirlwind out of the north (Ezek. 1:4). The psalmist wrote, "Promotion cometh neither from the east, nor from the west, nor from the south. But God is the judge" (Ps. 75:6, 7), as though the blessing of God comes from the north. Lucifer wanted to exalt his throne above the stars of God in the sides of the north (Isa. 14:13). When astronomers recently found a great empty place in the northern heavens, Christians were reminded that "[God] stretcheth out the north over the empty place, and hangeth the earth upon nothing" (Job 26:7).

If heaven has a recognizable shape, it is evidently a sphere. God is said to walk "in the circuit [circle, lit.] of heaven" (Job 22:14). How large is God's dwelling place? Its size is inconceivable, because the new Jerusalem will someday descend from God out of heaven, and that city will be nearly fifteen hundred miles in length, breadth, and height (Rev. 21:16).

The most important fact revealed about heaven is that it is the abode of God. In Isaiah we read that he inhabits eternity and that he dwells in the high and holy place (Isa. 57:15). We are accustomed to pray, "Our Father which art in heaven" (Matt. 6:9). God spoke to men from that place in Old Testament times (Exod. 20:22). His voice was heard from heaven in New Testament days when he said, "Thou art my beloved Son, in whom I am well pleased" (Mark 1:11). Solomon prayed, "Hear thou from heaven thy dwelling place" (2 Chron. 6:30). From there God looks down to behold all the sons of men, and from that holy place he hears the cries of his people (Ps. 33:13; 20:6). Christ dwelt in heaven before the incarnation; that is where he has been since his ascension. The Holy Spirit had his residence in that place prior to his coming to earth at Pentecost; he is referred to as "the Holy Ghost sent down from heaven" in 1 Peter 1:12.

Human language is not adequate for describing heaven. The closest thing to a description is found in such passages as Revelation 4:1-11, where John relates what he saw when he was called up away from the earth. But his terminology has confounded even the finest of minds. To fully comprehend his words we must wait until we too have been taken there. The first thing John saw was a throne, occupied by One who can be no other than God the Father. God's throne is frequently mentioned elsewhere in the Bible, e.g., "The Lord is in his holy temple, the Lord's throne is in heaven" (Ps. 11:4); Christ said, "Swear not at all; neither by heaven; for it is God's throne: nor by the earth; for it is his footstool" (Matt. 5:34, 35).

John saw a rainbow encircling the throne "in sight like unto an emerald" (Rev. 4:3). Before it was a crystal sea. Around it were twenty-four elders clothed in white and seated on twenty-four seats, or thrones, and wearing crowns of gold. Lightnings, thunderings, and voices proceeded out of the throne. Seven lamps of fire burned before it. "In the midst of the throne" John saw four living creatures. He described them as full of eyes and having six wings. Isaiah saw similar living creatures in his vision of the Lord sitting on his throne in a heavenly temple. He called them seraphim, or burning ones (Isa. 6:1-7).

This mention of a temple and an altar in heaven is one reason why the ancient Jews believed their places of worship were copies of what is in heaven. When God gave Moses instructions for building the furnishings of the tabernacle, he said, "Look that thou make them after their pattern, which was shewed thee in the mount" (Exod. 25:40; see also Heb. 8:5). Such revelations as these are mysterious to us. They are beyond our finite comprehension, but they give some idea of the holy, awesome place from which God rules the universe.

Heaven is also the home of the angels. When Christ was born, a heavenly host praised God in the skies above Bethlehem, then went back to their place in heaven (Luke 2:15). This promise was made to Nathaniel, "Hereafter ye shall see heaven open, and the angels of God ascending and descending upon the Son of man" (John 1:51). During the days of earth's tribulation, angels will come down from heaven to intervene in the affairs of men. They are mentioned over forty times in Revelation. They stand before God and they come out of the altar and the temple. An angel from heaven will bind Satan and cast him into the bottomless pit after the second coming of Christ (Rev. 20:1-3).

When Moses and Elijah appeared on the mount of transfiguration, fresh from the glory of heaven, they spoke with Christ about his forthcoming death in Jerusalem (Luke 9:31). This passage suggests that those who dwell in heaven may have knowledge of the future program of God on earth.

Christians are deeply interested in what their departed loved ones do between death and resurrection, and what we shall all be doing in the life to come. A search of the Scriptures reveals one remarkable answer. Instead of giving specifics, the Bible simply tells us how vastly different life will be from anything we experience now. In eternity "There shall be no more death, neither sorrow, nor crying, neither shall there be any more pain: for the former things are passed away. And he that sat upon the throne said, Behold, I make all things new" (Rev. 21:4, 5). We are told what will be missing rather than what will be present. Evidently human language can come no closer than this in describing what life with God will be like.

If the vocabulary of earth could portray what our activities in heaven will be, the Bible would certainly have told us more about it than it has. Knowing the former things will have passed away, we can be sure we shall know nothing of weariness, toil, or suffering. But our finite minds are unable to grasp all that will make up the abundant life of heaven.

The Scriptures do tell us that heaven is a place of unutterable joy. There is joy there now over one sinner who repents (Luke 15:7). When we are presented before the presence of Christ's glory, it will be with exceeding joy (1 Pet. 4:13; Jude 1:24). Paul was looking forward to that same day when he said his converts would be for him a crown of rejoicing (1 Thess. 2:19). There is to be singing in heaven such as never was heard on land or sea: "They sung a new song, saying, Thou art worthy to take the book, and to open the seals thereof: for thou wast slain, and has redeemed us to God by thy blood out of every kindred, and tongue, and people, and nation; . . . and we shall reign on the earth" (Rev. 5:9, 10). This is one of fourteen songs in the Book of Revelation, all of them sung in heaven by angels, by the elders, and by the redeemed.

Believers can begin to learn this heavenly song while they are still on the earth. When the word of Christ dwells in us richly, we sing with grace in our hearts to the Lord, "in psalms and hymns and spiritual songs" (Col. 3:16). Spirit-filled Christians are heavenly beings who sing and make melody in their hearts to the Lord (Eph. 5:18, 19). This is one of the true marks of spirituality.

Our hope is in heaven. The Bible speaks of "the hope which is laid up for you in heaven, whereof ye heard before in the word of the truth of the gospel" (Col. 1:5). We are begotten to a living hope (1 Pet. 1:3). We "lay hold upon the hope set before us: which hope we have as an anchor of the soul, both sure and stedfast" (Heb. 6:18, 19). Every instructed Christian is "looking for that blessed hope, and the glorious appearing of the great God and our Saviour Jesus Christ" (Titus 2:13). Like other revelations about heaven, this has a practical, present-day value. It leads to separation from sin: "Every man that hath this hope in him purifieth himself, even as he is pure" (1 John 3:3).

Rewards are waiting in heaven for Christians. Christ said, "Great is your reward in heaven" (Matt. 5:12). He exhorted his disciples to lay up for themselves treasures in heaven (Matt. 6:20). The Gospels tell of rewards awaiting those who suffer reproach, those who give a cup of cold water in his name, those who leave all to follow him (Matt. 10:42; 19:28), and those who show love to their enemies (Luke 6:35). The Epistles mention the granting of future rewards for enduring trials, keeping the faith, winning souls, keeping the precepts of the Word, feeding the flock, and being an example to others.

The names of believers are written in heaven. When the seventy unnamed disciples expressed joy because the demon world was subject to them in Christ's name, the Lord told them to rejoice instead because their names were written in heaven (Luke 10:17-20). He will confess us by name before his Father (Matt. 10:32). The Book of Revelation is a rich storehouse of information about those whose names are in the Lamb's book of life. They will never see or worship the beast, they will escape the lake of fire, they will have a place in the new Jerusalem, and their names will never be blotted out. Paul mentioned the fact his coworkers' names were written

182

there (Phil. 4:3). Christians who have missed being memorialized in the Westminster Abbeys of the world will not miss being enrolled in heaven, a privilege the majority of people on earth know nothing about.

We have an inheritance in heaven, "incorruptible, and undefiled, and that fadeth not away, reserved in heaven for you" (1 Pet. 1:4). This truth is distinct from the doctrine of rewards. Because we are children of God, we are "heirs of God, and joint-heirs with Christ" (Rom. 8:17). Our inheritance awaits us in God's dwelling place, where nothing can touch it or deprive us of it. Our heavenly treasure may be said to consist of the rewards God will graciously give for faithful service, plus an unearned inheritance given for the sole reason that we are his children through faith in Jesus Christ. Somewhere in the universe, above the stars, every believer has great wealth which cannot be corrupted or defiled or touched by time. Such revelations provide a wonderful incentive to godly living.

"Our citizenship is in heaven, from which also we eagerly await for a Savior, the Lord Jesus Christ" (Phil. 3:20, NASB). On earth we are strangers and pilgrims with no certain abiding place; but we have been born into the family of heaven (Eph. 3:15). Some day we will be translated to that sweet country, beyond the clouds and beyond the tomb, where our true citizenship is, and where Christ awaits the time of our arrival. We have been born again as citizens of that place. This implies obligation and duty. The knowledge that we belong to a heavenly land brings with it the responsibility for actions befitting our destiny. We partake of a heavenly calling. Our deeds on earth, and the principles which guide us, should honor and bring glory to the country we represent as ambassadors.

Heaven is our true home. At death we shall be absent from the body and present with the Lord in glory (2 Cor. 5:6-8), as we go to our "long home" (Eccles. 12:5). We are to be forever with the Lord and with our heavenly family, as members of the household of God.

This theme has held special appeal to several hymn writers, who looked forward to heaven as the home of the soul after their trials on earth were ended. Among the scores of hymns once heard in churches everywhere, the immortal words of Bernard of Cluny will be remembered by many:

> *O sweet and blessed country, the home of God's elect!*
> *O sweet and blessed country that eager hearts expect!*
> *Jesus, in mercy bring us to that dear land of rest;*
> *Who art, with God the Father, and Spirit, ever blest.*

Children of the heavenly King once loved to sing:

> *We are traveling home to God, in the way our fathers trod;*
> *They are happy now, and soon we their happiness shall see.*

PART IV
FINAL DESTINY

CHAPTER 19
THE FINAL SEVEN YEARS

The last few years before Christ's second advent will be the most terrifying period in human history. Many names and descriptive phrases are given to this short interlude. The Lord called it the "great tribulation" (Matt. 24:21). The prophet Joel referred to it as "destruction from the Almighty" (Joel 1:15). It is "the indignation" of Daniel 11:36 and "the hour of trial" of Revelation 3:10. For Israel it will be "the time of Jacob's trouble" (Jer. 30:7). For the Gentile nations it will be a time of unparalleled distress (Luke 21:25). It will bring great changes to the earth after the worst earthquake in history (Rev. 16:18). When the wrath of God has spent itself, vast multitudes will have perished (Isa. 24:6). These and other revelations have left their mark on the traditions of countless nations. Ancient records everywhere on earth declare that human history will conclude with divine judgment.

In descriptions of the tribulation, the Bible speaks of smoke, fire, brimstone, great hail, lightning, darkness, and evil beasts. Stars will fall; the earth will be terribly shaken. Man's long effort to govern himself will come to a climactic end amid sights never before witnessed on land or sea. The throne of God will dominate the stage. Voices and trumpet blasts will issue from heaven. Plagues will be visited on the human race. The supernatural will burst in upon the earth. Angels and demons will become active. The bottomless pit will be opened. Frightful signs will become visible to men. Fearful announcements will be made from the sky. The world will face "a time of trouble, such as never was since there was a nation even to that same time" (Dan. 12:1). Nothing like it will ever occur again (Matt. 24:21).

Why should God introduce such a time of trouble just prior to Christ's return? The prophetic Scriptures give us at least four reasons. Prominent among them is God's purpose "to punish the world for their evil, and the wicked for their iniquity" (Isa. 13:11). Later in the same book this purpose is reiterated: "Behold, the Lord cometh out of his place to punish the inhabitants of the earth for their iniquity" (Isa. 26:21). All nations will have to drink the cup of the fury of the Lord, including "all the kingdoms of the world, which are upon the face of the earth" (Jer. 25:26). Men will try to hide, but there will be no escape from the divine judgments (Rev. 6:15-17).

A second reason has to do with the people of Israel. During the time of tribulation God will call a "remnant" of his people back to himself and prepare them for their place of leadership in the coming kingdom. He will refine them as silver is refined, and try them as gold is tried (Zech. 13:9). It is not his primary purpose to discipline the Jews at that time; they have known his chastening hand for many centuries. The Jews will pass through dark days with all others living at that time, but their trials will be tempered with mercy: "I will correct thee in measure, and will not leave thee altogether unpunished" (Jer. 30:11). God will extend to them the loving invitation, "Come, my people, enter thou into thy chambers, and shut thy doors about thee: hide thyself as if it were for a little moment, until the indignation be overpast" (Isa. 26:20).

A third reason for the tribulation is God's plan to prepare a company of people who will populate the earth during the millennial kingdom. Men do not easily learn obedience to God. Thus, when trouble and affliction become widespread, there will be a greater readiness on the part of many to heed the message being proclaimed everywhere, the gospel of the kingdom (Matt. 24:14). Many people will emerge from the tribulation cleansed by the blood of the Lamb (Rev. 7:9-14). Christ will welcome into his kingdom all who have shown themselves ready: "Come, ye blessed of my Father, inherit the kingdom prepared for you from the foundation of the world" (Matt. 25:34).

A fourth reason is found in God's purpose to prepare the universe for the kingdom of his Son. God will remove mountains, cause islands to disappear, and level the rough country (Rev. 16:20; Zech. 14:10). After he shakes the heavens and the earth, astonishing changes will take place. The light of the sun will increase (Isa. 30:26). Springs will break out in desert places. Infertile ground will yield crops. Illness and deformity will no longer plague the human race (Isa. 35:1-7). The devil and his hosts will be bound and imprisoned, bringing to an end the evils which have troubled the world ever since Satan introduced sin in the garden of Eden.

The most detailed accounts of the tribulation appear in the Book of Revelation. Three groups of divine judgments are set forth, seven in each group. They begin with a scene in heaven. The Lamb will take a book, or scroll, from the Father and open its seals, one by one. As each seal is broken, a divine judgment will be sent to the earth. The first four will introduce the four horsemen of the Apocalypse. When the first one rides forth, bloodless conquest will take place under the Antichrist. The next three will bring war, famine, and death. One quarter of the world's inhabitants will perish. The fifth seal will introduce martyrdom, the sixth will bring a great earthquake and dreadful sights in the sky. The seventh seal will prepare the way for another series of severe and extensive judgments associated with the sounding of seven angelic trumpets (Rev. 5, 6).

As the first angel sounds his trumpet, hail and fire will destroy one-third of all the earth's vegetation. When other angels blow their trumpets, a third part of the sea will become blood red, a third of its creatures will die, and a third of the world's shipping industry will be destroyed. A burning star will fall from heaven, turning one-third of all rivers and streams bitter and causing many to die. A third of the sun, moon, and stars will become dark. The bottomless pit will be opened; it will belch forth thick smoke. Out of the smoke will come flying insects. For five months they will torment men with painful stings. Another trumpet will release four angels who are bound in the Euphrates River, and with them, an army of two hundred million will appear. They will kill a third of the human race.

After the seven angels have sounded their trumpets, seven vials (bowls) of the wrath of God will be poured out on the earth. Loathsome and malignant sores will break out on the followers of the Antichrist. The sea will become blood red, killing every creature in it. All fresh water will become like blood. The heat of the sun will increase to the point where men are scorched. Darkness will descend on the throne and kingdom of the beast. Men will gnaw their tongues in pain. The river Euphrates will dry up to prepare the way for an invasion by the kings of the east. A tremendous earthquake will take place. Cities will be destroyed, islands removed from their places, and mountains destroyed. Great hailstones will fall from the sky.

As these terrible events follow one another, two witnesses sent by God will proclaim his message to the people of the earth. They will be given power to destroy their enemies with fire, to prevent the rain from falling, to turn waters into blood, and to smite the earth with plagues. Three and a half years after the two witnesses begin their ministry, they will be killed by the beast. Their dead bodies will lie in the streets of Jerusalem for three and a half days. Then a voice will call from the sky and they will stand on their feet and ascend to heaven in the sight of their enemies (Rev. 11:3-12).

After a great war in heaven, Satan and his angels will be cast into the earth. Then the beast (the Antichrist) will rise from the sea. The devil will give him power, a throne, and great authority. The beast will receive a deadly wound by a sword. He will be healed, and live (a miracle mentioned three times in the same chapter—Rev. 13:3, 12, 14). The world will worship him and Satan.

A second beast will come up "out of the earth" (Rev. 13:11); this phrase may also be rendered, "out of the land," and possibly refers to Palestine. It is possible, therefore, that this beast, also called "the false prophet" (19:20), will be a Jew. He will be given power to perform miracles. His greatest miracle will be to give breath to a man-made image of the first beast. All who refuse to worship the image will be killed. The false prophet, primarily a religious leader subservient to the first beast, will require everyone to receive a mark on their right hands or foreheads. He will take control of the world economy by issuing an edict that no one may buy or sell without the mark.

One of the best known statements in the Book of Revelation occurs at this point: the first beast is a man, and his number is 666.

Three kinds of wrath will wreak havoc on the earth. First, the wrath of God will cause men to run to the wilderness, saying to the mountains and rocks, "Fall on us, and hide us from the face of him that sitteth on the throne, and from the wrath of the Lamb: for the great day of his wrath is come, and who shall be able to stand?" (Rev. 6:16-17). Second, "Woe to the inhabitants of the earth and of the sea! for the devil is come down unto you, having great wrath, because he knoweth that he hath but a short time" (12:12). Third, the wrath of men will have free rein to cause strife (Prov. 15:18). All forms of wickedness are restrained during the present age. When that restraint is gone, the fury of wicked men will be added to the wrath of God and of the devil. "In those days shall men seek death, and shall not find it; and shall desire to die, and death shall flee from them" (Rev. 9:6).

After the true church is taken to heaven, apostate ecclesiastical organizations and unsaved church members will become part of an ecumenical monstrosity, a world religious system called "MYSTERY, BABYLON THE GREAT, THE MOTHER OF HARLOTS AND ABOMINATIONS OF THE EARTH" (Rev. 17:5). It will be identified with "that great city, which reigneth over the kings of the earth" (17:18). "That great city" refers to a city of seven hills or mountains (17:9), a familiar historical description of Rome.

This evil religious system will be so closely associated with the Antichrist that it is depicted as an unclean woman riding the beast. Later the ten nations under the beast's control will turn against Mystery Babylon and destroy it. The beast then will become a world dictator and will demand to be worshipped by all.

Revelation also contains an extended prophecy about the great city Babylon (Rev. 18), widely regarded as a symbolic reference to the demonic commercial system of the tribulation. God will destroy this Babylon near the end of the final seven years, before the Lord returns. The Book of Revelation presents a striking contrast between Babylon, the wicked mistress of the beast ruler, and the holy bride of Christ, who will reign with him over the millennial kingdom.

Israel is mentioned often in Scriptures dealing with the tribulation. In fact, the first time tribulation is mentioned in the Bible is when Moses refers to the latter days when the Jews, who are scattered among the nations, find themselves "in tribulation" (Deut. 4:30). When they seek the Lord and begin to honor him, he promises to deliver them. Some of the details of this deliverance appear in Deuteronomy 30:1-10. When the Jews of the world honor the Lord, he will return, gather them from among the nations, bring them into their own land, bless them, and judge their enemies. This chronology is confirmed by many other prophecies (e.g., see Jer. 30:7-11).

God never leaves the world without a witness. During the tribulation he will choose servants from the twelve tribes of Israel—12,000 from each tribe, for a total of 144,000 (Rev. 7:4-8). At this point in the prophecy Scripture speaks of the appearance of "a great multitude, which no man could number, of all nations, and kindreds, and people, and tongues" (7:9). These will be "they which came out of great tribulation" (7:14). Some people believe this refers to a vast heavenly throng; others understand the text to indicate that this multitude will emerge from the tribulation to live on earth during the kingdom of Christ.

The event which signals the beginning of the final seven years will be the signing of a treaty between "the prince that shall come"—the Antichrist—and the Jewish people then living in the land (Dan. 9:26, 27). After three and a half years, the Antichrist will break the treaty and turn against the Jews. The abomination of desolation will be put in the holy place in Jerusalem. The temple sacrifices will cease, and all Jewish people who heed the words of Christ will flee from Judaea.

Meanwhile, the devil will be cast into the earth and will begin a terrible persecution of the Jews. Two-thirds of all Jews will perish, and one-third will pass through fiery trials (Zech. 13:8, 9). The Jewish people are told, "He that shall endure unto the end, the same shall be saved" (Matt. 24:13). This is not a formula for salvation from sin. It is a promise that all righteous Jews who survive the tribulation will enjoy the blessings of the kingdom, along with the great multitude of Gentile believers.

Other prophecies supply further details about the Hebrew nation during the tribulation. Ezekiel devotes two chapters to an invasion of the land of Israel by a northern confederacy, and the divine destruction of the invading hordes (Ezek. 38, 39). Joel tells of an assembly of Jews who cry to God for help at that time (Joel 2:12-20). Malachi speaks of the coming of Elijah (Mal. 4:5). Zechariah describes the attack on Jerusalem by all nations after the city has become "a burdensome stone for all people" (Zech. 12:3). He says the Lord will go forth from heaven and deliver his ancient people. The Jews will recognize him as Jesus, the pierced One, and mourn for him in the bitterness of their discovery (12:10). The Gospels likewise refer to Jews living during the final years.

The climax of the tribulation is depicted in a series of dramatic scenes. Three unclean spirits like frogs will come forth from the dragon, the beast, and the false prophet. They will "go forth unto the kings of the earth and of the whole world, to gather them to the battle of that great day of God Almighty" (Rev. 16:14). The nations will gather together at Armageddon.

In that day, the nations will attack Jerusalem. They will take the city, capturing half of its population. At this point Christ will suddenly appear, and he will go forth to battle. Heaven will open and Christ will descend with all the armies of heaven (Zech. 14:2-5; Rev. 19:11-21). His feet will touch down on the Mount of Olives, just east of Jerusalem. An earthquake will divide the mount into two parts, producing a great valley through which the people of the city will make their escape. "The beast, and the kings of the earth, and their armies" (Rev. 19:19) will try to overcome the returning Lord. But the beast will be taken, together with the false prophet. They will be cast alive into a lake of fire burning with brimstone.

The final seven years of life as we know it will come to an end with this victory over the beast. Christ will then sit on the throne of his glory to judge the nations. His ancient people will be regathered from all over the earth and restored to their promised land. With all evil men purged from the world, the devil and his angels bound, and the earth transformed, earth's golden age will dawn at last.

CHAPTER 20
THE TWO BABYLONS

Babylon is among the most significant cities in the Bible. It is mentioned nearly three hundred times. In Babylon a great rebellion occurred during the early years of the human race. It led to the confusion of tongues. The times of the Gentiles began there when God made Nebuchadnezzar a world ruler, and will continue until Babylon has been destroyed. One-eighth of the Book of Revelation deals with Babylon.

The references to Babylon in Revelation 17 and 18 contain striking differences. One chapter speaks of a harlot, the other of a great city. In chapter 17 the beast and his ten kings destroy the harlot; in chapter 18 "the kings of the earth" bewail the fall of the great city. The harlot is evidently a symbol; but nothing in chapter 18 suggests the city is in any way symbolic. The best approach to these two chapters is to regard them as a double revelation, presented in two distinct parts which emphasize two different aspects of Babylon.

The most important key to these chapters is found in the word *mystery* (Rev. 17:5). In the New Testament, *mystery* often means a freshly revealed truth. "Mystery, Babylon" is therefore a new revelation about Babylon, unknown to the Old Testament writers.

In Revelation 17 an angel shows the apostle John a great harlot, sitting on a scarlet beast. She is dressed in purple, scarlet, and precious stones. On her forehead a name is written: "MYSTERY, BABYLON THE GREAT, THE MOTHER OF HARLOTS AND ABOMINATIONS OF THE EARTH" (17:5). What does she represent? The text provides several explanations. She is called the mother of harlots and abominations; hence, she has a religious character. Jerusalem was called a harlot after it became unfaithful to God (Isa. 1:21-23). Tyre and Nineveh are both called harlot cities for similar reasons (Isa. 23:15-17; Nah. 3:4). The Old Testament uses the word "abominations" for gross sins (e.g., Lev. 18:26), and also in reference to the images Israel worshipped when she turned away from God (Ezek. 7:20).

Secular history teaches that after Nimrod founded Babylon (Gen. 10:10), it became the fountainhead of world idolatry. The great empires embraced this false religion. In John's day, the city of Rome was the center of the Babylonian religion. Its images were as prominent as the idols of Egypt under the Pharaohs.

The Mystery Babylon of Revelation 17 is generally understood to be the idolatrous religions of the ages, combined in a world religion supported by the Antichrist during the first half of his rule. The headquarters of this religious system may well be the city of Rome. The harlot religion will take over the Roman Catholic Church. Apostate Protestantism will also form a part of it, as will other world religions. When the time has come for the Antichrist to direct all worship toward himself, he and his ten kings will destroy Mystery Babylon, and the greatest idol since the days of Nebuchadnezzar will stand in the holy place of the Jewish temple in Jerusalem (Rev. 13:14, 15).

The textual explanations of the meaning of the harlot make it clear that it is a city, as well as a worldwide religious system. "The woman which thou sawest is that great city, which reigneth over the kings of the earth" (Rev. 17:18). The only city answering to this description in John's day was Rome, capital of the Empire. We also read that the harlot will sit on seven mountains (17:9); Rome was once known as the city of the seven hills. The imperial coins of the Roman Empire depicted the capital as a woman seated on seven hills. The apostle Peter applied the name "Babylon" to Rome (1 Pet. 5:13).

Protestant and Roman Catholic commentators agree that the city of Revelation 17 was pagan, idolatrous Rome. After all, it was a Roman edict that brought Mary to Bethlehem for the birth of Christ. Rome crucified him, destroyed the city of Jerusalem, scattered the Jews abroad over the earth, and persecuted the early Christians. A widely accepted belief is that the Roman Empire will reappear in history during the last days, in the form of ten countries subject to the Antichrist.

The harlot will ride the beast in the last days. This means she will be supported by the Antichrist and his ten kings. Later in the tribulation he and his kings will destroy Mystery Babylon, and the worship of the beast will be introduced.

With Mystery Babylon gone from the scene, the city of Babylon will take the center of the stage. Some Christians think the city of chapter 18 is the same city mentioned in Revelation 17:18. They point to the volcanic character of Italy as an indication that Rome could indeed be destroyed by an eruption, as was Pompeii.

"That great city Babylon" (Rev. 18:10) will be a great commercial center, wealthy and beloved by world leaders, but it will be exceedingly sinful. It evidently stands near a great river or sea. There is nothing in the text to suggest this is not a literal city.

There are many contrasts between chapters 17 and 18. Different angels speak in each case, and at different times. The beast and his ten kings are said to destroy the *harlot,* but the kings of the earth bewail the destruction of the *city.* There is no reference to the beast and his kings in chapter 18. The time of the destruction of the *harlot* is during the final seven years, while the *city* is not destroyed until the end of that period. No one laments the end of the harlot, but monarchs, merchants, and mariners mourn the burning of the *city.* In chapter 18 God's people are warned to come out of the city; no such warnings appear in chapter 17.

Several details about the great city are repeated several times. The suddenness of her destruction is mentioned four times; there are also four references to the people who stand far off to watch the smoke of her burning. There are three references to the divine character of this judgment. Several passages make it clear the city will perish forever. And it is possible that the repetition found in the words, "Babylon the great is fallen, is fallen" (Rev. 18:2), refers to the destruction of both a world religious system and a great city.

Much has been written about this double prophecy in Revelation. Following are three items, taken from various sources, which may shed some light on these revelations. They are presented without comment.

1. Over the centuries many have believed that the ancient city of Babylon will be rebuilt at the end of the age. Certain Old Testament prophecies are cited in support of this view. It is pointed out that "the burden of Babylon" is associated with the day of the Lord in Isaiah 13, and that when Babylon perishes it "shall be as when God overthrew Sodom and Gomorrah" (Isa. 13:19). This is interpreted to mean that the city must be destroyed in the same manner as were the cities of the plain. Revelation 18:21 is also cited as proof, as are verses from Jeremiah 51. Historical facts are used to show that the ancient city was not destroyed suddenly, but that it gradually decayed over an extended period.

2. A possible interpretation of a strange prophecy in Zechariah 5:5-11 is that it predicts the future removal of the headquarters of latter-day idolatry from Rome to the land of Shinar, where Babylon stood. In this prophecy an angel showed the prophet an *ephah*, a measure somewhat like a bushel basket, containing a woman called "Wickedness." Two other women with stork-like wings lifted up the *ephah* between earth and heaven. When Zechariah asked where they were taking it, the angel replied, "To build it an house in the land of Shinar: and it shall be established, and set there upon her own base" (5:11). It has been suggested the woman in the *ephah* is the same woman of Revelation 17. In the past, her base of operations has been moved from Babylon to Pergamos and then to Rome, and it may be moved again. The world headquarters of idolatrous religion could therefore be reestab-

lished in the place where ancient Babylon stood on the plain of Shinar. A modern Babylon may be built some day.

3. Historian Arthur J. Toynbee made a surprising comment about Babylon in *Civilization on Trial* (New American Library). Upon observing that the center of gravity of human affairs is determined largely by geography, that is, the distribution of peoples with their energy and skills, he wrote, "Ultimately their gravitational pull may then draw the center point of human affairs . . . to some locus approximately equidistant from the western pole of the world's population in Europe and North America, and its eastern pole in China and India, and this would indicate a site in the neighborhood of Babylon, on the ancient portage across the isthmus between the Continent and its peninsulas of Arabia and Africa."

CHAPTER 21
THE SECOND COMING
OF CHRIST

The promised return of Christ to the earth is the most important theme of unfulfilled prophecy. This event will be the great
watershed dividing the history of the world into two eras.
Satan has dominated life on earth ever since the garden of
Eden: Christ will be in total control after he comes back to
reign. The first prophetic words in man's history were uttered
by Enoch. They refer not to the incarnation, but to the second
coming of Christ with myriads of his saints (Jude 1:14). The
last promise of the Bible is, "Surely I come quickly." It is
followed by the last prayer, "Even so, come, Lord Jesus" (Rev.
22:20).

In view of the significant biblical emphasis on Christ's return, it is surprising that the doctrine of the second coming
was lost to the church for centuries, until its recovery near the
end of the nineteenth century. It is the only doctrine at which
men will scoff in the last days (2 Pet. 3:3, 4).

Everyone who has read the Bible knows it speaks of two
comings of Christ. He came the first time as a baby to
Bethlehem. He came "to minister, and to give his life a ransom
for many" (Mark 10:45), "to seek and to save that which was
lost" (Luke 19:10), and to destroy the devil and his works
(Heb. 2:14; 1 John 3:8). After he had provided salvation by
his death and resurrection, he ascended to heaven to await the
time of his return. "This man, after he had offered one sacrifice
for sins for ever, sat down on the right hand of God; from
henceforth expecting till his enemies be made his footstool"

(Heb. 10:12, 13). Extensive prophecy tells how he will come a second time to take his power and reign.

The two comings are sometimes mentioned together in a single text. "Christ was once offered to bear the sins of many; and unto them that look for him shall he appear the second time without sin unto salvation" (Heb. 9:28). Isaiah gave us the familiar words, "Unto us a child is born, unto us a son is given." The child was born to die; the Son will bear the government of the world on his shoulder after he appears (Isa. 9:6). Christ came the first time "to proclaim the acceptable year of the Lord"; he will return for "the day of vengeance of our God" (Isa. 61:2). At the annunciation, the angel Gabriel spoke of both comings: At the first advent, Mary was to conceive and bring forth a son; at the second advent, "the Lord God shall give unto him the throne of his father David: and he shall reign over the house of Jacob for ever, and of his kingdom there shall be no end" (Luke 1:32, 33).

The Bible contains much more revelation about the second coming than the first. Many of the details regarding the incarnation were purposely made obscure, and could only be understood fully in the light of the historical fulfillment. The apostle Peter stated that the Old Testament prophets did not understand the meaning of what was written about the two appearings. They inquired and searched diligently, "searching what, or what manner of time the Spirit of Christ which was in them did signify, when it testified beforehand the sufferings of Christ, and the glory that should follow" (1 Pet. 1:11).

In retrospect, however, we see that the place and time of his advent were plainly revealed. The Messiah would be born in the city of Bethlehem in Judaea (Mic. 5:2), 483 years after Artaxerxes' commandment to restore and rebuild the city of Jerusalem (Dan. 9:25; Neh. 2). That is a date known to historians. Daniel gives this time period as "seven weeks, and threescore and two weeks." These weeks are *heptads,* or periods of seven years each, totalling 483 years altogether. This was the exact length of time between the decree to rebuild Jerusalem and the day the Lord entered Jerusalem to be crucified. In contrast with this clear prediction about the time of his first advent, we know very little about the time of his return: "Of that day and hour knoweth no man, no, not the angels of heaven, but my Father only" (Matt. 24:36).

There are numerous contrasts between the two appearings. Christ came once in lowliness and meekness as the Lamb to be slain; he will come again in power and glory as the Lion of the tribe of Judah to crush his enemies. Once he was rejected by men; someday he will be their Judge. He was born in obscurity; his second coming will be as startling and public as a flash of lightning. He came the first time to die for men's sins; he will return to punish sin. His first advent introduced the present age; his second advent will occur after its close. The Jewish people were scattered all over the world after his first coming; Christ will regather them from all nations after he comes again. When he was born in Bethlehem the Roman Empire was at its height; when he returns a western confederacy of nations will have taken its place. He came the first time to win for himself a bride; he will come again with his bride by his side.

As we have seen, it is a mistake to consider the rapture of the church a part of the second coming. These events are totally unrelated, except in that one must precede the other. At the rapture Christ does not return to the earth; he descends only to the air to meet his bride. When he returns he will come with his saints. At the rapture the movement will be upward; when he returns the movement will be downward.

Teaching about the second coming permeates all of Scripture. It was continually on the lips of Christ. Angels spoke of it. The apostles emphasized it. Many such texts are familiar. Paul said believers are going to appear with Christ in glory (Col. 3:4). James wrote, "The coming of the Lord draweth nigh" (James 5:8). Peter mentioned the promise of his coming (2 Pet. 3:3, 4). To Jude it was revealed that "The Lord cometh with ten thousands of his saints" (Jude 1:14). John gave us the great text, "Behold, he cometh with clouds; and every eye shall see him" (Rev. 1:7). Similar declarations abound. There are over 318 New Testament passages which speak of the second coming.

Many names and titles in reference to the Lord are used in passages dealing with the second advent. They are so numerous and so striking that they can be arranged in a way that provides a summary of what happens when he returns. As the "Word of God," the Lord will smite the nations at Armageddon (Rev. 19:13-15). As the "stone cut out without hands," he is going to destroy Gentile world government (Dan. 2:44, 45). He will be known as the "anointed son" when he ascends the holy hill of Zion (Ps. 2:2-7). As the "Jehovah" of the Old Testament, he will come and regather the scattered people of Israel and bless them in their ancient land (Deut. 30:3-5). He will rule them as their "Governor" (Matt. 2:6). As their "Deliverer" he will remove their sin (Rom. 11:26).

Saints on earth will see him as the heavenly "Bridegroom" returning from the marriage of the Lamb (Matt. 25:1-6; Luke 12:36). He comes as the "Sun of righteousness with healing in his wings" for all mankind (Mal. 4:2). He will stand for an ensign of the people as the "root of Jesse," drawing men to himself as the fountain of salvation (Isa. 11:10). He will rule the world in righteousness as "King of kings and Lord of lords" (Rev. 19:16). He will bring an end to earth's dark night, for he is the "bright and morning star" (Rev. 22:16). Wars will cease to the ends of the earth when he comes bearing the name "Prince of Peace" (Ps. 46:9; Isa. 9:6).

Although no date has been revealed for his return, we know it will be after God has completed forming the church. God visited the Gentiles the first time "to take out of them a people for his name. And to this agree the words of the prophets; as it is written, After this I will return, and will build again the tabernacle of David, which is fallen down; and I will build again the ruins thereof, and I will set it up" (Acts 15:14-16). There is no specific time element here, but we are given the divine order of events. There are other such indications. We are to be kept from the hour of trial which is to try the whole world (Rev. 3:10), so we know that, before the Lord returns, the great tribulation must run its seven-year course after the rapture.

The first mention of the return of the Lord is found in Moses' address to the Israelites given on the plains of Moab before they entered the promised land. He says that someday the Jewish people, scattered among all nations, will remember their tragic history, return to the Lord, and obey his Word. When that happens the Lord will turn to them in compassion. Moses gives this promise to Israel: "[He] will return and gather thee from all the nations, whither the Lord thy God hath scattered thee" (Deut. 30:3).

Although the Scriptures are silent on the time of Christ's return, we do know precisely *where* he shall appear at his return. In Zechariah 14:3, 4 we are informed that "his feet shall stand in that day upon the mount of Olives, which is before Jerusalem on the east." Nothing could be more specific.

Another description of the second coming relates it to Armageddon. The apostle John saw heaven opened and the Lord coming forth to "judge and make war." When he comes, the battle of the great day of God Almighty will be at its height, from the plain of Esdraelon to Jerusalem and Edom (Rev. 16:13-16). Christ's return will bring an end to Armageddon as he defeats the nations and their leader, the beast. He will return to the same place from which he ascended, the Mount of Olives, and deliver the people of Israel in Judaea and Jerusalem.

The most complete outline of events leading to his return was given by Christ himself in his Olivet Discourse: "Immediately after the tribulation of those days shall the sun be darkened, and the moon shall not give her light, and the stars shall fall from heaven, and the powers of the heavens shall be shaken: and then shall appear the sign of the Son of man in heaven: and then shall all the tribes of the earth mourn, and they shall see the Son of man coming in the clouds of heaven with power and great glory" (Matt. 24:29, 30). In the words of Mark, Christ will come "in those days, after that tribulation" (Mark 13:24).

In Luke 21:25-27 Christ speaks of signs by which believers of that day will know his coming is near: "There shall be signs in the sun, and in the moon, and in the stars; and upon the earth distress of nations, with perplexity; the sea and the waves roaring; men's hearts failing them for fear, and for looking after those things which are coming on the earth: for the powers of heaven shall be shaken. And then shall they see the Son of man coming in a cloud with power and great glory." Matthew 24 adds to this list. Israel's birthpangs will begin with wars, famines, pestilences, and earthquakes (Matt. 24:6-8). The gospel of the kingdom will be preached in all the world; the abomination will stand in the holy place; the great tribulation will come and run its course; heavenly signs will be followed by the sign of the Son of man in heaven. This list could be greatly extended by what is revealed elsewhere.

With so many plain statements about Christ's promised return, it is incredible to learn of various attempts to interpret them figuratively. Some commentaries have sought to prove that the second coming took place at the destruction of Jerusalem in A.D. 70; they confuse the wrath of the Roman armies visited on the city with the future display of the wrath of God. Others have suggested that the Lord returned on the day of Pentecost, mistaking the descent of the Holy Spirit for the second coming of Christ, and overlooking the fact that some prophecies of Christ's return were written years *after* Pentecost. Some liberals claim that Christ never intended to return in person, and that the promises have to do only with a "spiritual presence" among his people.

It cannot be denied that the Scriptures plainly state Christ will come back to the earth personally and visibly in his resurrected and glorified body. When a cloud obscured him from the sight of the disciples at his ascension, they were told, "This same Jesus, who is taken up from you into heaven, shall so come in like manner as ye have seen him go into heaven" (Acts 1:11). John wrote, "Behold, he cometh with clouds, and every eye shall see him" (Rev. 1:7). He will come suddenly (Matt.

24:27). His return will be unexpected. "In such an hour as ye think not the Son of man cometh" (24:44). He will be "revealed from heaven with his mighty angels, in flaming fire taking vengeance on them that know not God, and that obey not the gospel of our Lord Jesus Christ" (2 Thess. 1:7, 8). "The brightness of his coming" will destroy the Antichrist (2 Thess. 2:8). When he appears, the people of Israel will recognize him as the pierced One, Jesus of Nazareth, and will mourn over their rejection of him (Zech. 12:10).

The reason for the Lord's second advent is made clear in passages having to do with the church, Israel, the nations, and the unseen world. He must return to fulfill his promise that the church is going to reign with him on the earth (Rev. 5:10). He will come to deliver the Jews from their enemies. He will regather the children of Israel from the nations where they have been dispersed, judge them in "the wilderness of the people" (Ezek. 20:35), purge out the rebels, and restore the righteous to the promised land (see 20:34-38). His return is necessary so that all Israel can be saved, as he turns away ungodliness from Jacob (Rom. 11:26). He must raise his people at the resurrection of the just (Dan. 12:2). His rebuilding of the tabernacle of David demands his return, as does his sitting on the throne of his father David to reign over the house of Jacob forever. He must return to pour out the Holy Spirit on all flesh, and to fulfill all the ancient covenants he has made with the Jews.

The second coming of Christ is necessary because the Gentile nations must be dealt with. When he appears, all the earth's nations will attempt to make war with the Lord and his Anointed, saying, "Let us break their bands asunder, and cast away their cords from us" (Ps. 2:3). Christ will shatter and consume the nations of the end time. Then he will sit in judgment on them, invite the righteous to enter the kingdom, and cast the wicked into everlasting fire (Matt. 25:31-46).

At the second coming, nature will be transformed. A great earthquake will change the face of the earth. The curse will be lifted, and the world will become a paradise. Creation itself will be "delivered from the bondage of corruption into the glorious liberty of the children of God" (Rom. 8:21).

The unseen world of evil spirits will cease to have any part in the life of the human race. Satan, who has been the god of this world for thousands of years, will be bound, as will his demon host. With the church triumphant, Israel saved, the nations judged, and creation delivered from centuries of pain and misery, the kingdom of Christ will begin. It will last a thousand years.

CHAPTER 22

THE DESTINY OF SATAN

The popular notion that Satan is a grotesque being who inhabits a fiery hell is a far cry from the way the Bible describes him. Christ spoke of him often. He is mentioned by Paul, Peter, James, John, and Jude. He bears many titles and names. He is "the serpent," "the old dragon," "the devil," the "prince of this world," the "prince of the power of the air," and the "prince of the demons." He is called Lucifer, Belial, Beelzebub, Abaddon, and Apollyon.

The first prophecy recorded in Scripture was addressed to Satan: Some day the Seed of the woman—Christ—will bruise the head of the serpent. This enigmatic expression refers to the ultimate doom of the devil.

One of the most illuminating prophecies about the final end of Satan is found in Ezekiel 28. The chapter begins with an address by God to the prince of Tyre; this ruler's destiny was to die and descend to Sheol. He is regarded as a type of Antichrist because the language of 28:2 ("Thou hast said, I am a God, I sit in the seat of God.") is referred to in 2 Thessalonians 2:4.

The address to the prince of Tyre is followed by an address to the king of Tyre. Most Bible students believe the description of the king of Tyre is a revelation concerning Satan. Some have believed "the king of Tyre" is simply another name for the devil. Others have seen this as a revelation of the motivating force behind the wickedness of the prince of Tyre, just as there were satanic forces behind the rulers of Persia and Greece (Dan. 10:13-20).

The king of Tyre is identified as "the anointed cherub that covereth" (Ezek. 28:14), a Bible term used exclusively of angelic beings (e.g., 1 Sam. 4:4; Ezek. 10:1). In his primal state, his work was to cover, or protect. He was possibly one of the guardians of the throne of God. The exalted position of this angelic being is seen in the fact that during a dispute about the body of Moses, Michael the archangel dared not to bring a railing accusation against him, but said simply, "The Lord rebuke thee" (Jude 1:9).

This being was on the holy mountain of God. He walked in the midst of the "stones of fire." He had been in Eden, the garden of God (evidently a heavenly rather than an earthly place, because it is associated with the stones of fire). The Lord said to him, "Thou sealest up the sum, full of wisdom, and perfect in beauty" (Ezek. 28:12); this is an indication that he was the wisest and most beautiful of all God's creatures. Satan was perfect until iniquity was found in him—he became proud of his beauty and brightness. Because of his sin, he will be cast out of the mountain of God, brought down to the earth, and finally destroyed.

Another Old Testament prophecy about Satan's destiny is found in Isaiah 14:12-17, where he is addressed as Lucifer, or "light-bearer." Lucifer said in his heart, "I will ascend into heaven, I will exalt my throne above the stars of God: I will sit also upon the mount of the congregation, in the sides of the north: I will ascend above the heights of the clouds: I will be like the most High" (14:13, 14).

No matter how wise and powerful Lucifer may be, such presumption could lead only to judgment. God pronounced his doom: "Thou shalt be brought down to hell [Sheol, lit.], to the sides of the pit" (Isa. 14:15). Sheol, sometimes translated "hell" in the Old Testament, is the Hebrew name for a place of confinement in the heart of the earth where the enemies of God are imprisoned. Lucifer will someday be cast into the bottomless pit, the pit of the abyss (Rev. 20:1). His descent into the region of the damned will be seen by other inhabitants who have preceded him. They will exclaim, "Is this the man that made the earth to tremble, that did shake kingdoms; that made the world as a wilderness, and destroyed the cities thereof; that opened not the house of his prisoners?" (Isa. 14:16, 17).

The most graphic and complete predictions of Satan's future appear in the Book of Revelation. In the latter days there will be war in heaven between Michael and his angels and the "dragon" and his angels. Michael will prevail. The devil will then be cast out into the earth, his angels with him (Rev. 12:7-17). Christ spoke of this when he said, "I beheld Satan as lightning fall from heaven" (Luke 10:18).

Satan has always had access to the presence of God. He was among the angels who presented themselves before the Lord in Job's day (Job 1:6). He attacked Job at that time and he has been accusing and attacking humanity ever since (Rev. 12:10). This will come to an end when Michael vanquishes him in the middle of the years of tribulation (Dan. 9:27). At that time the devil will empower the Antichrist (2 Thess. 2:9; Rev. 13:2) who, in turn, will begin his great persecution of the Jews (Rev. 12:13-17).

Satan's final burst of activity among men and demons will culminate in Christ's victory over the forces of evil at his second advent. An angel will come down from heaven bearing the key to the bottomless pit and a great chain. He will lay hold of "the dragon, that old serpent, which is the Devil, and Satan," and bind him a thousand years (Rev. 20:1-3). There he will remain, bound and powerless, while Christ reigns on the earth for a thousand years. When the time comes for him to be loosed for "a little season," he will go out to deceive the nations one final time, gather the rebellious of the kingdom age, and lead them against the beloved city of Jerusalem, world capital during the millennium. God will send fire from heaven to devour these armies. Satan will finally be cast into the lake of fire. His long career will end in the place God has prepared for him.

Scripture contains a series of prophecies concerning the demons. The origin of this host of evil spirits is not clear. They are believed to be fallen angels who shared in Lucifer's rebellion against God. It has been suggested that they form a company one-third the size of the angelic host, for the dragon's tail "drew the third part of the stars of heaven" in the vision seen by John (Rev. 12:3, 4). If the demons are indeed Satan's angels, then they too will be cast into the lake of fire (Matt. 25:41).

The demons have always known about their ultimate fate. When Christ met two demon-possessed men in the country of the Gergesenes, the evil spirits cried out, "What have we to do with thee, Jesus, thou Son of God? art thou come hither to torment us before the time?" (Matt. 8:29). The future time of which they spoke refers to the great day when the earth will be shaken and the kings of the earth judged (Isa. 24:20-23). At that time the Lord will punish "the host of the high ones that are on high" (24:21), as well as earthly kings.

Another group of fallen angels, distinct from the demons, is already imprisoned. They were locked up because they sinned in a manner likened to that of Sodom and Gomorrah (Jude 1:7). They were cast down to a place called Tartarus in the Greek text of 2 Peter 2:4, and bound with chains. Tartarus is evidently a special region in Hades reserved for these wicked beings. After being bound for thousands of years they will be released and judged at that great day when the demons of the present age, now free but yet to be taken and imprisoned, will be released to receive their eternal sentence of doom. Knowing the certainty of their fate, they believe, and tremble (James 2:19).

CHAPTER 23
THE SECOND COMING
OF THE HOLY SPIRIT

The second coming of Christ is a familiar theme in Bible prophecy, but few have heard of the second coming of the Holy Spirit. Most works on theology and doctrine neglect the important place the Spirit will have in the end times. Revelation about his second coming is largely confined to the Old Testament, because it is related primarily to the coming of the kingdom of Christ. It is usually described as an "outpouring," the word used of his coming at Pentecost (Acts 10:45).

When Christ left heaven to become incarnate, the whole universe was moved. A new star appeared. Angels burst the bands of their invisibility to announce his coming. The glory of God was seen by men for the first time in six hundred years. Satan and the world of demons became active. Prophecies which had stood for centuries were fulfilled. Teaching was heard on earth, and manifestations of deity were seen such as had not been witnessed since the dawn of history.

After Christ left the earth, another major event in the divine program occurred. The Holy Spirit arrived. Christ had mentioned the coming of the Spirit at least seven times. He had even declared it was expedient for him to go away so the Comforter could come (John 16:7). The greatest missionary text in the Bible anticipates it: "Ye shall receive power, after that the Holy Ghost is come upon you: and ye shall be witnesses unto me both in Jerusalem, and in all Judaea, and in Samaria, and unto the uttermost part of the earth" (Acts 1:8). The Spirit came to occupy a human temple—the church—for an entire age. There are fourteen references to this fact in the New Testament, beginning with John 7:39: "This spake he of the Spirit, which they that believe on him should receive: for the Holy Spirit was not yet given; because that Jesus was not yet glorified."

In ancient times the Spirit had come on men for special ministry (e.g., Judg. 3:10), filling them for particular tasks (Exod. 31:3), but he never dwelt on earth until the day of Pentecost. On that day the confusion of tongues, begun at Babel, was reversed in measure when the disciples spoke in the diverse languages of the assembled multitude. A new divine program was introduced. God began to form the company of people destined to be the bride of Christ and to reign with him forever. Peter wrote long afterward of "the Holy Ghost sent down from heaven" (1 Pet. 1:12).

When the Holy Spirit finally leaves the earth after his purposes for this age have been accomplished, dramatic events will take place. The world will lose all its Christians as they are translated to heaven. The Spirit's work of convicting the world of sin will give way to the sending of strong delusion to those who have rejected Christ (2 Thess. 2:11). Supernatural restraint on evil will cease. The man of sin will be revealed. The people of Israel will be restored to God's favor. The world will be ready for the Antichrist and Armageddon.

The Holy Spirit will perform various functions immediately prior to his departure from the earth at the end of the present age:

1. He will warn against apostasy. "The Spirit speaketh expressly, that in the latter times some shall depart from the faith, giving heed to seducing spirits, and doctrines of devils" (1 Tim. 4:1). When this takes place, the great apostasy described elsewhere in the New Testament will have come to Christendom. Men will turn away from the truth proclaimed for centuries and accept demonic teachings.

2. The Spirit will plead with the churches. In Revelation 2, 3 the following warning appears seven times: "He that hath an ear, let him hear what the Spirit saith unto the churches.

Similar admonitions are to be found throughout the epistles. Believers are reassured that they need not fear the wrath of God to be poured out during the tribulation period. Christ gave the promise, "I . . . will keep thee from the hour of temptation, which shall come upon all the world, to try them that dwell upon the earth" (Rev. 3:10). Earthdwellers must face the terrors of that time, but the church will have been raptured to heaven.

3. The Spirit will bring to an end his restraint of evil. "The mystery of lawlessness is already at work; only he who now restrains will do so until he is taken out of the way" (2 Thess. 2:7, NASB). The Holy Spirit's presence on earth holds back the tide of wickedness that would otherwise overwhelm the human race. When he leaves, "then shall that Wicked be revealed, whom the Lord shall consume with the spirit of his mouth, and shall destroy with the brightness of his coming" (2:8). The time word "then" is important. It makes clear that the Antichrist will not be recognized until *after* the Holy Spirit has left.

4. At the rapture, the Spirit will give life to the dead in Christ. God will "quicken your mortal bodies by his Spirit that dwelleth in you" (Rom. 8:11). As Christ descends from heaven to call his church away, the Holy Spirit will give life to sleeping believers and they will rise from the dead. Afterward he will be active on earth, as in Old Testament days. When God's two witnesses are killed by the Antichrist, the Spirit will enter into them, and they will rise and ascend to heaven (Rev. 11:11, 12).

5. The Spirit will escort the bride of Christ to meet her heavenly Bridegroom in the air. "He [God by his Spirit] which raised up the Lord Jesus shall raise up us also by Jesus, and shall present us with you" (2 Cor. 4:14; see also Rom. 8:11). He will never leave his temple (John 14:16).

As he leaves the earth, the Spirit will abandon nonbelievers to their wickedness and to the judgment of God. Wrath will be poured out, as fire fell on Sodom.

The Bible does not reveal how long the Spirit of God will

be in heaven before he comes to earth for the second time. It is clear his return will follow the seven years of tribulation. Possibly there will be an interval between the rapture of the church and the beginning of the time of earth's travail. The common assumption that the departure of the church marks the beginning of the tribulation is erroneous. No Scripture teaches this.

There are several reasons why the Holy Spirit must depart. The church—his temple—will be taken away. The appearing of the Antichrist cannot take place until he is gone, nor can the wrath of God be poured out while he and the church are present. He has "delivered us from the wrath to come" (1 Thess. 1:10); "God hath not appointed us to wrath" (5:9). It is impossible for the world to receive the Holy Spirit. Only his temple—the church—can receive him (John 14:17).

When will the second coming of the Holy Spirit take place? It would be enough to say that it will be when Christ appears with his saints in glory (Col. 3:4), but the Old Testament is specific about it. The Holy Spirit will return after the Jews have returned to their ancient land and have suffered an invasion from the north (Ezek. 39:28, 29). His return will precede the changes in nature, which occur prior to the establishment of the kingdom of Christ (Isa. 32:13, 15).

Scripture tells us of five specific activities of the Holy Spirit upon his return to the earth:

1. He will make God's words known. "I will pour out my spirit unto you, I will make known my words unto you" (Prov. 1:23). "A famine . . . of hearing the words of the Lord" is to come some day (Amos 8:11), to be followed by a time when "the earth shall be full of the knowledge of the Lord, as the waters cover the sea" (Isa. 11:9). The coming of the Holy Spirit will make the difference. As he makes God's words known to the people of Israel, they will become the Lord's witnesses (43:12), taking the place of Christian believers as ministers of God (61:6).

2. He will make the earth fruitful. When God cursed the earth, the ground began to bring forth thorns and thistles, as

it does today (Gen. 3:17, 18). But the curse will end with the Holy Spirit's return. "Upon the land of my people shall come up thorns and briers; . . . until the spirit be poured upon us from on high, and the wilderness be a fruitful field" (Isa. 32:13-15). All of nature will be transformed. "The desert shall rejoice, and blossom as the rose. . . . The eyes of the blind shall be opened, and the ears of the deaf shall be unstopped. Then shall the lame man leap as an hart, and the tongue of the dumb sing" (35:1-6).

3. He will satisfy the thirsty with the blessing of God. "For I will pour water upon him that is thirsty, and floods upon the dry ground: I will pour my spirit upon thy seed, and my blessing upon thine offspring" (Isa. 44:3). The outpouring of the Spirit is synonymous with God's blessing. The longings of mankind will be satisfied.

4. He will restore the Jews to divine favor. "Neither will I hide my face any more from them: for I have poured out my Spirit upon the house of Israel" (Ezek. 39:29). The unveiled face of God was enjoyed by the people of Israel for centuries. When God turned his face away from his people because they persisted in sin, godly Jews felt it keenly. They prayed, "Turn us again, O God, and cause thy face to shine; and we shall be saved" (Ps. 80:3).

5. He will bestow the gift of prophecy. "And it shall come to pass afterward, that I will pour out my spirit upon all flesh; and your sons and your daughters shall prophesy, your old men shall dream dreams, your young men shall see visions" (Joel 2:28). This is written at the close of the divine revelation about an invasion of the land and God's destruction of the invaders (2:20). When Peter quoted this passage on the day of Pentecost, he did not say Joel's prophecy had been fulfilled. The Spirit had been outpoured on the believers assembled in an upper room, but not on all flesh (Acts 2:1-21).

There are obvious parallels between what the Spirit will do at his second coming and what he brought to the church at his first coming. To a limited extent, the Spirit already fulfills the functions listed above.

Because the Holy Spirit is now resident in the church, we do not have to wait for the coming of the future kingdom of Christ to witness many of the wonders of that longed-for time. Every Christian now experiences a taste of the countless blessings of that future age when the Spirit will be poured forth in all his fullness.

CHAPTER 24
EARTH'S GOLDEN AGE

Men have always longed for a paradise on earth, where the human race would live in happiness and prosperity in a world devoid of sickness or sorrow. Plato expressed his concept of a perfect city in *The Republic.* Sir Thomas More wrote about an imaginary island blessed with an ideal social and political state. He called his book *Utopia,* which means "no place" in Greek. The term has come to be used as a synonym for any place or state of ideal perfection.

While dreamers have been singing and writing about beautiful isles of nowhere, they have ignored the Bible's description of a golden age that will be introduced to the earth. Scripture devotes more space to it than to any other prophetic theme. The revelation is vast and surprisingly complete. We are told when and how it will come, much about its ruler and subjects, how it will affect the human race, the animal kingdom, the world of nature and the unseen world, how long it will continue, and how it will finally end.

This "golden age" is the earthly kingdom of the Lord Jesus Christ. It is a theme of prophecy altogether different from God's sovereign rule over the universe. It should not be confused with the invisible kingdom of God into which people are introduced by the new birth. During the golden age the Lord will rule the world literally and visibly, from his throne in the city of Jerusalem.

This is not a doctrine based on a few isolated texts. Although the best-known chapter dealing with it is Revelation 20—

which reveals Christ will reign for a thousand years—the complete doctrine of the golden age can be developed from the Old Testament alone.

The coming of the kingdom will mean God's original purposes for the earth can be realized. When the curse is lifted, a groaning creation will rejoice in its deliverance; the children of God will have their day. With the imprisonment of Satan, the evil principles and influences governing ungodly men will vanish, and people will be solely responsible for their actions. All the promises God has given over many centuries will be fulfilled. The dreams of God's people will be realized. Christ will be vindicated and glorified in the place where he was rejected and crucified. Good will triumph over evil, and righteousness will reign.

When will this kingdom be established? The prophet Hosea places it in the latter days: "For the children of Israel shall abide many days without a king, . . . afterward shall the children of Israel return, and seek the Lord their God, and David their king; and shall fear the Lord and his goodness in the latter days" (Hos. 3:4, 5). Isaiah's famous description indicates it is to come in "the last days" (Isa. 2:2). Daniel was told God will set up a kingdom after the days when ten kings rule under the Antichrist (Dan. 2:44). Jeremiah says it will occur after the trouble Jacob will experience in the great tribulation (Jer. 30:7-9). Such passages make it clear we are reading about an actual, visible kingdom.

The New Testament is in perfect accord with these Old Testament revelations. Matthew supplies an outline of events which places the kingdom after the tribulation and after the personal return of Christ to the earth (Matt. 24:39; 25:31). In Revelation, after the seventh angel sounds his trumpet, the announcement is made, "The kingdoms of this world are become the kingdoms of our Lord, and of his Christ; and he shall reign for ever and ever" (Rev. 11:15). The millennial reign is to follow the doom of the beast, the binding of Satan, and the first resurrection (20:6): "they . . . shall reign with him a thousand years."

How will the kingdom come? Scripture indicates it will be introduced suddenly, by an act of God, to the accompaniment of catastrophic changes in the world. It will be like a great stone smiting the nations of the earth and breaking them in pieces, so that "no place was found for them," as Daniel describes it (Dan. 2:35). The Lord will send forth angels to "gather out of his kingdom all things that offend" (Matt. 13:41). Then he will sit on the throne of his glory to separate the wicked from the righteous as the kingdom begins (25:31). He will regather the elect of Israel from all over the earth (Jer. 23:7, 8).

In an irresistible work of divine sovereignty, God will set his King on the holy hill of Zion (Ps. 2:6). Suddenly the heavens will open and the King will arrive on earth to vanquish his foes and take his throne (Rev. 19:11).

The name of this coming King is revealed in Luke 1:31-33: "Thou . . . shalt call his name JESUS. He shall be great, and shall be called the Son of the Highest: and the Lord God shall give unto him the throne of his father David: and he shall reign over the house of Jacob for ever; and of his kingdom there shall be no end."

He will be the Jehovah of the Old Testament, as announced by the prophets long ago. "The days come, saith the Lord, that I will raise unto David a righteous Branch, and a King shall reign and prosper, and shall execute justice and judgment in the earth. In his days Judah shall be saved, and Israel shall dwell safely: and this is his name whereby he shall be called, THE LORD OUR RIGHTEOUSNESS" (Jer. 23:5, 6). This Branch—the Lord—will sit and rule on his throne; he will build the temple of the millennium (Zech. 6:12, 13). He is to be both divine and human. Born of a virgin, he will be called "Immanuel" (Isa. 7:14), or "God with us." He will have come out of the city of Bethlehem, he "that is to be ruler in Israel" (Mic. 5:2).

The Bible specifies the spot where his throne will be placed: "At that time they shall call Jerusalem the throne of the Lord; and all the nations shall be gathered unto it, to the name of the Lord, to Jerusalem: neither shall they walk any more after the imagination of their evil heart" (Jer. 3:17). The Lord calls the city "the place of my throne, and the place of the soles of my feet, where I will dwell in the midst of the children of Israel for ever" (Ezek. 43:7). His throne is called the "throne of David" (Isa. 9:7). Jerusalem will sing in that day because "the king of Israel, even the Lord, is in the midst of thee" (Zeph. 3:15).

Christ will be given the throne by the Father, with "dominion, and glory, and a kingdom, that all people, nations and languages, should serve him" (Dan. 7:14). Associated with him will be princes, nobles, judges, counselors, and other rulers (Isa. 1:26; 32:1; Jer. 30:21). David will have a part in the kingdom. The people "shall serve the Lord their God, and David their king, whom I will raise up unto them" (Jer. 30:9). "Out of Zion shall go forth the law, and the word of the Lord from Jerusalem" (Isa. 2:3).

There will be universal peace, joy, holiness, and justice. "The earth shall be filled with the knowledge of the glory of the Lord, as the waters cover the sea" (Hab. 2:14). The disciples will receive a place of honor. Jesus said to them, "Ye which have followed me, in the regeneration when the Son of man shall sit in the throne of his glory, ye also shall sit upon twelve thrones, judging the twelve tribes of Israel" (Matt. 19:28). This fulfills the word given to Isaiah: "I will restore thy judges as at the first" (Isa. 1:26). The kingdom will also have a constitution (Matt. 5–7).

Who will populate the earth during the kingdom? Scripture often speaks of the regathering of righteous Jews and their restoration to the land of their fathers, where their Messiah will rule over them. At the beginning of the millennium there will be few of them, because of the severe persecutions of the tribulation, in which two-thirds will have died. During the course of the millennium, however, they will multiply until they become like the sand of the sea "which cannot be measured nor numbered" (Hos. 1:10). They will become the leading nation of the world under the Messiah (Deut. 28:13). They will be a blessing to all nations instead of a curse (Zech. 8:13). Gentiles will seek them out because God is with them (Zech. 8:23). The Jewish people will be God's chosen witnesses in the earth (Isa. 43:10). "Israel shall blossom and bud, and fill the face of the earth with fruit" (Isa. 27:6).

Gentiles who have survived the great tribulation will complete the population of the world in the kingdom. "When the Son of man shall come in his glory, and all the holy angels with him, then shall he sit upon the throne of his glory: and before him shall be gathered all nations" (Matt. 25:31, 32). After judging them, the Lord will say to the righteous, "Come, ye blessed of my Father, inherit the kingdom prepared for you from the foundation of the world" (25:31-34). Another description of this scene is found in Matthew 13:41-43. "All things that offend" (13:41) will be gathered out of his kingdom and cast into a furnace of fire. "Then shall the righteous shine forth as the sun in the kingdom of their Father" (13:43). Zechariah says, "It shall come to pass, that every one that is left of all the nations which came against Jerusalem shall even go up from year to year to worship the King, the Lord of hosts" (Zech. 14:16).

These and other passages tell us no unsaved person will enter the kingdom as it begins. We read of a great multitude of people "of all nations, and kindreds, and people, and tongues" who come out of the great tribulation. They are saved people who "have washed their robes, and made them white in the blood of the Lamb" (Rev. 7:14). Some have assumed this multitude is made up of believers who died during the tribulation, and have gone to heaven. But the text is better understood as referring to the great company of people who survive the day of vengeance to live on the earth during the millennium. Daniel indicates the kingdom will belong only to saved individuals: "The greatness of the kingdom under the whole heaven, shall be given to the people of the saints of the most High" (Dan. 7:27).

The prophecy that every wicked person will be cast out as the kingdom dawns is not undisputed. Some texts seem to contradict this: Psalm 72:9, for example, says the Lord will have enemies during this time; Revelation 12:5 declares the Lord will rule with a rod of iron. But this textual problem is solved by the revelation that children will be born during the kingdom who will resent Christ's rule. As the population of the world explodes during the Edenic conditions of Christ's reign, many of those who are born will yield only feigned or pretended obedience (see Ps. 18:44). This has been true of every age. Regenerated parents do not always have saved progeny.

Old Testament saints and the church will have important positions in the coming kingdom of Christ. Christians are told plainly they will occupy Christ's throne with him (Rev. 3:21), they will reign with him (2 Tim. 2:12), and they are to reign on the earth (Rev. 5:10). Furthermore, all who have a part in the first resurrection are to reign with Christ for a thousand years (20:6). This is clear enough, but no details are supplied as to the exact nature of our reign. We do know where we shall reside; the Lord promised to prepare a place for us (John 14:3), believed to be the new Jerusalem, which will come down from God out of heaven (Rev. 21). It is a definite place, not merely a state of being. This future city is called "the Lamb's wife," and the names of the apostles are found in it, as are the names of the twelve tribes of Israel. Hebrews 12:22 calls it "the heavenly Jerusalem," and includes among its occupants the church and "the spirits of just men made perfect" (12:23), understood to be the Old Testament saints. In this celestial city will live the saints of Old and New Testament days. They will reign on the earth, but they will not *live* on the earth.

We look in vain for any statement in Scripture about whether we will be visibly present on the earth during the kingdom age. Our ministry during the kingdom can apparently be accomplished without the necessity for our physical presence on earth. The ministry of angels is not visible to the eye—our work in reigning with Christ may be similar to theirs. The earthdwellers of that time will certainly occupy their natural bodies, but it is not necessary to assume that resurrected and glorified people from previous ages will mingle with those who are still in the flesh. There is nothing inherently impossible in such a concept, however, because Christ walked the earth in his glorified body after his resurrection for forty days.

Much of the Scripture dealing with the coming kingdom is devoted to the dramatic changes that will occur everywhere in creation. They will affect the human race, the animal kingdom, nature, and the unseen world of spirits. Man's lifespan will be greatly extended: "As the days of a tree are the days of my people, and mine elect shall long enjoy the work of their hands" (Isa. 65:22). Longevity will be comparable to that of the patriarchs who lived before the flood, when life expectancy approached one thousand years. The death of a person at age one hundred will be looked upon as the death of a child (65:20). Death will not be banished until the dawn of eternity (1 Cor. 15:26). With the curse removed there will be no sickness (Isa. 33:24). "The eyes of the blind shall be opened, and the ears of the deaf shall be unstopped. Then shall the lame man leap as an hart, and the tongue of the dumb sing" (35:5, 6). The aging process will continue, so old men will still need staffs or canes for help in walking (Zech. 8:4). There will be joyful wedding parties (Jer. 33:11), and boys and girls will play in the streets or parks of the cities (Zech. 8:5).

A study of all that is revealed about life in the golden age shows people will marry, have children, and get old. They will work, sing, play, worship, and fall into sin. Some will rebel against the Lord. Men will operate farms, keep sheep, go fishing, build and repair homes, and engage in manufacturing. They will travel by highway and by ship. They will serve God, bear witness for him, and offer sacrifices in the temple at Jerusalem. They will eat, drink, sleep, and live in houses. There will be cities and nations.

Men will rebuild the old wastes, raise up the former desolations, and repair the wasted cities and the desolations of many generations (Isa. 61:4). "Men shall buy fields for money, and subscribe evidences, and seal them" (Jer. 32:44). People will own houses, fields, and vineyards. Private property will be respected: "They shall sit every man under his vine and under his fig tree; and none shall make them afraid" (Mic. 4:4). The waste cities will be filled with flocks of men (Ezek. 36:38). It will be a world of work, and not idleness (Isa. 65:22).

Peace will be universal: "He maketh wars to cease unto the end of the earth" (Ps. 46:9). "Nations shall not lift up sword against nation, neither shall they learn war any more" (Isa. 2:4). There may possibly be a universal language: "Then will I turn to the people a pure language" (Zeph. 3:9). Unprecedented prosperity will follow; national wealth will be diverted from munitions to peaceful pursuits.

The nature of animals will be changed: "In that day will I make a covenant for them with the beasts of the field, and with the fowls of the heaven, and with the creeping things of the ground" (Hos. 2:18). When the natural world becomes what it was before the curse, preying animals will lose their ferocity. "They shall not hurt nor destroy in all my holy mountain: for the earth shall be full of the knowledge of the Lord, as the waters cover the sea" (Isa. 11:9). Children will lead lions about; the king of beasts will eat straw like the ox (11:7). Wolves will dwell with lambs, leopards with kids, lions with calves (11:6). The enmity between serpents and the human race will disappear. No one will fear harmful beasts. People "shall dwell safely in the wilderness, and sleep in the woods" (Ezek. 34:25).

The creation will be transformed. Under a brighter sun and moon, trees will grow in the place of thorns and briers. Rainfall will increase (Ezek. 36:25). There will be rivers in high places and fountains in the midst of valleys. Lakes and pools of water will grace the barren wilderness. The dry land will be refreshed by springs of water (Isa. 41:18). Rivers and streams will flow down every hill and mountain (30:25). "In the wilderness shall waters break out, and streams in the desert" (35:6).

There will be no change in the order of day and night. "While the earth remaineth, seedtime and harvest, and cold and heat, and summer and winter, and day and night shall not cease" (Gen. 8:22). The fertility and productivity of the soil will become so remarkable that a handful of corn or wheat planted in an unlikely place will produce fruit like a forest (Ps. 72:16). There will be vineyards and gardens (Isa. 65:21). "Behold, the days come, saith the Lord, that the plowman shall overtake the reaper, and the treader of grapes him that soweth seed; and the mountains shall drop sweet wine" (Amos 9:13). Land once desolate will become like the garden of Eden (Ezek. 36:35).

The greatest change of all, however, will take place in the unseen world. Demons will be eliminated. These beings who have long controlled nations, caused men to commit atrocities, started wars and destruction, and brought untold misery to the human race will be gathered together and imprisoned in the abyss for the duration of the kingdom (Isa. 24:21, 22). They know their time is coming, and they fear that day. When demons first recognized Christ they cried out, "Art thou come hither to torment us before the time?" (Matt. 8:29). "The demons . . . believe, and tremble" (James 2:19).

Satan has deceived the nations, shaken kingdoms, and made the world a wilderness (Isa. 14:16, 17). After the Lord comes, an angel will take the devil, bind and cast him into the abyss, and place a seal on him. There he will stay for a thousand years, while the glorious kingdom of Christ is enjoyed on the earth. After the thousand years have ended, God will have one final use for the devil. Satan will be loosed from his prison, "and shall go out to deceive the nations which are in the four quarters of the earth, Gog and Magog, to gather them together to battle: the number of whom is as the sand of the sea" (Rev. 20:8). When this host attacks the saints and the beloved city, fire will come down from God out of heaven and devour them. The devil will be cast into the lake of fire, the dead of all the ages will be judged at the great white throne, and with earth's golden age a thing of the past, eternity will dawn.

CHAPTER 25
THE NEW JERUSALEM

Revelation's description of the new Jerusalem is enough to startle even the most vivid imagination. In spite of all the books written about the Book of Revelation, little light has been cast on the passage (Rev. 21:9-27). Some commentaries have tried to handle the text by boldly declaring that the literal fulfillment of John's vision is "manifestly impossible." Others take it as it stands, but their best efforts to explain it fail to add much to our understanding of the future city of God. Nevertheless, a few observations about the text may help to bring it into clearer perspective.

The new Jerusalem is often contrasted with mystery Babylon. Each city is introduced by "one of the seven angels which had the seven vials" (Rev. 17:1; 21:9). Babylon is likened to an unclean woman; Jerusalem is the chaste bride of the Lamb. Babylon is the habitation of every foul spirit; Jerusalem is the home of angels and saints. Babylon defiles every nation involved with it; Jerusalem radiates its glory on every nation walking in its light. Evil Babylon will be destroyed; holy Jerusalem will endure forever.

In Revelation 21, John first tells how he was captivated by the brilliance of the light of the place he saw in his vision. Then he describes the most astonishing city to be found anywhere in literature. It descends from God out of heaven. Awesome in its size, it is surrounded by a great and high wall, with three gates on each of its four sides. The gates are of pearl. The walls are of jasper, a green precious stone shot through with many other colors. The twelve foundations are garnished with jewels, the streets are gold in color but transparent like glass. The city has no need of the sun or moon because it is illuminated by the glory of God and the Lamb.

The size of the new Jerusalem is much larger than any metropolis ever conceived by man. Its walls are 216 feet high. The city itself is nearly 1500 miles long on each side, and nearly 1500 miles high. Some idea of the vast size of what John saw in his vision is conveyed by thinking of the new Jerusalem in relation to the United States. If placed over America, it would reach from New York to Denver and from Maine to Florida. It would cover more than half the territory of the United States. If the eternal city is conceived of as suspended in the sky 10,000 miles above the earth, it would appear to be twenty times as large as the moon, which is 2,160 miles in diameter in an orbit 238,000 miles above the earth.

The only information we have about the shape of the city is that it is "foursquare" and that "the length and the breadth and the height are equal" (Rev. 21:16). Bible scholars have thought of it as a cube, a sphere within a cube, or a pyramid. It is easier to think of a river flowing from the throne of God down the sides of a pyramid than those of a cube, and it is easier to conceive of a wall surrounding a pyramid than a cube or a sphere.

Who will occupy the new Jerusalem? Revelation includes the bride, the Lamb's wife, angels, and the children of Israel; The Lord God and the Lamb are also associated with it. These are identical with the occupants of "the heavenly Jerusalem" as described by Paul in Hebrews 12:22-24. He speaks of the general assembly and church of the firstborn, an innumerable company of angels, the spirits of just men made perfect (believed to be Old Testament saints), God the Judge of all, and Jesus the mediator of the new covenant.

It is evident that the three divisions of the human race described in 1 Corinthians 10:32—the Jew, the Gentile, and the church of God—will continue into eternity. God promised long ago to the Jewish people, "As the new heavens and the new earth, which I will make, shall remain before me, saith the Lord, so shall your seed and your name remain" (Isa. 66:22). The nations, or Gentiles, "shall walk in the light of it: and the kings of the earth do bring their glory and honour into it" (Rev. 21:24). The church, the bride of the Lamb, is to be so intimately associated with the new Jerusalem that the two are inseparable.

One of the most wonderful aspects of John's vision of the new Jerusalem is that God himself will make it his home. After he makes all things new, his tabernacle, or habitation, will be "with men, and he will dwell with them" (Rev. 21:3). The God who has always seemed to be so far from the world of sin will at last be at rest in his eternal city, together forever with the people he saved.

CHAPTER 26
ETERNITY:
THE END OF TIME

The word "eternity" appears only once in the King James Version of the Bible. In Isaiah 57:15 God is called "the high and lofty One that inhabiteth eternity." But related words, such as "eternal," "everlasting," "forever," are used hundreds of times. Everlasting life, mentioned only once in the Old Testament (Dan. 12:2) is spoken of over forty times in the New Testament. According to prophecy, an everlasting king will exercise everlasting dominion over an everlasting kingdom, in everlasting light. The dark side of eternity is seen in reference to everlasting punishment, destruction, fire, burnings, chains, and confusion.

The Hebrew word used most often to express the idea of eternity is *olam*. Its Greek counterpart is *aion*. These ancient words, however, are not precisely equivalent to the English word "eternity." *Olam* and *aion* mean "time out of mind," or "an incalculable period of great remoteness." The fact that there is no English parallel for these words has posed problems in Bible translations. In one place we read of "the earth which he hath established for ever" (Ps. 78:69); in another it is stated that "the earth . . . shall perish" (102:25, 26). But there is no contradiction in the original languages. God established the earth for a vast period of time, incomprehensible to us, but when it has run its course, the earth will be burned up (2 Pet. 3:10) and pass away (Rev. 21:1). The impermanence of the present earth is implied in Genesis 8:22: "While the earth remaineth, seedtime and harvest, and cold and heat, and summer and winter, and day and night shall not cease."

Much has been revealed about what we may call eternity past. The Bible takes us back to the beginning, before the creation of the world. When God brought the world into existence by the word of his power, "the morning stars sang together, and all the sons of God shouted for joy" (Job 38:7).

Most of what is written about eternity past has to do with Jesus Christ. "In the beginning was the Word, and the Word was with God, and the Word was God" (John 1:1). No sooner is this revelation given—about a beginning which antedates that of Genesis 1:1—than we are told, "All things were made by him; and without him was not any thing made that was made" (John 1:3). The fact that Christ was the Creator of the universe is repeated several times. "The world was made by him" (1:10). God "created all things by Jesus Christ" (Eph. 3:9), "by whom also he made the worlds" (Heb. 1:2). "By him were all things created, that are in heaven, and that are in earth, visible and invisible, whether they be thrones, or dominions, or principalities, or powers: all things were created by him, and for him" (Col. 1:16).

Before the foundation of the world Christ was with God, rejoicing always before him in glory (Prov. 8:22-26). He participated in the framing of the plan of the ages. After his incarnation he uttered "things which have been kept secret from the foundation of the world" (Matt. 13:35). He will fulfill part of that eternal plan when he invites the righteous nations to "inherit the kingdom prepared for you from the foundation of the world" (25:34).

After he created the universe, he was active in it: "[His] goings forth have been from old, from everlasting" (Mic. 5:2). The apostle Peter wrote of Christ as "a lamb without blemish and without spot: who verily was foreordained before the foundation of the world" (1 Pet. 1:19, 20). Revelation 13:8 states that he is "the Lamb slain from the foundation of the world."

The election of Christians took place in eternity: We are "elect according to the foreknowledge of God" (1 Pet. 1:2). "He hath chosen us in him before the foundation of the world"

(Eph. 1:4). We have been "predestinated . . . unto the adoption of children by Jesus Christ to himself" (Eph. 1:5). Eternal life was promised to us before the world began (Titus 1:2). Our names were written in the book of life from the foundation of the world (Rev. 17:8). Even the good works to which we have been called were "before ordained that we should walk in them" (Eph. 2:10). We are recipients of the grace of God "which was granted us in Christ Jesus from all eternity" (2 Tim. 1:9, NASB).

Scripture contains a number of statements about the eternal plan of God, which includes Christians with all creation. "The Lord of hosts hath sworn, saying, Surely as I have thought, so shall it come to pass; and as I have purposed, so shall it stand. . . . For the Lord of hosts hath purposed, and who shall disannul it?" (Isa. 14:24, 27). "My counsel shall stand, and I will do all my pleasure: . . . I have spoken it, I will also bring it to pass; I have purposed it, I will also do it" (46:10, 11).

That plan called for the creation of the earth as the theater of the universe, upon which would be enacted the drama of sin and salvation (see 1 Cor. 4:9 in the original Greek text). God created it to be inhabited (Isa. 45:18). He placed man upon it and human history began to move on toward its appointed consummation. Second Thessalonians 2:13, 14 teaches that believers bridge the gap between eternity past and eternity future: "God hath from the beginning chosen you to salvation through sanctification of the Spirit and belief of the truth: whereunto he called you by our gospel, to the obtaining of the glory of our Lord Jesus Christ." In the plan of God, our beginning is found in the ancient past when we were chosen; our future includes participation in the glory of Christ throughout eternity.

When future ages have dawned at last, most Bible prophecy will have been fulfilled. Christ will have reigned on earth for a thousand years. Satan will have been imprisoned and cast into the lake of fire. The unjust will have been raised from the dead at the resurrection of the unjust to stand before the great white throne for judgment.

Most of what is revealed about eternity future is contained in the Bible's final two chapters. Earth and heaven will pass away. There will be no more sea. A new heaven and a new earth will be created. The holy city will come down from heaven. God will make all things new, and he will dwell among men. "His servants shall serve him" (Rev. 22:3). There will be no more death, sorrow, crying, or pain. All things will be made new. There will be no night and no need for the sun, because the glory of God and the Lamb will provide the light. The curse will be lifted from the earth. A pure river of water of life will proceed from the throne of God and of the Lamb.

As we enjoy an inheritance that will never pass away (1 Pet. 1:4) in the presence of God, things of the past "shall not be remembered, nor come into mind" (Isa. 65:17). The Son of God will rule over an everlasting dominion (Dan. 2:44). His eternal relationship to the Father will continue, "that God may be all in all" (1 Cor. 15:28).

Israel will continue through eternity as a distinct people. If the ordinances of the sun and moon "depart from before me, saith the Lord, then the seed of Israel also shall cease from being a nation before me for ever" (Jer. 31:36). "For as the new heavens and the new earth, which I will make, shall remain before me, saith the Lord, so shall your seed and your name remain" (Isa. 66:22).

The Gentile nations "which are saved shall walk in the light" of the new Jerusalem, and bring their glory and honor into it (Rev. 21:24-26). Saints of past ages will be present, "the spirits of just men made perfect," with an innumerable company of angels (Heb. 12:22, 23).

The unsaved will enter the dark side of eternity. They will be condemned to everlasting fire and everlasting torment. "Their worm shall not die, neither shall their fire be quenched; and they shall be an abhorring unto all flesh" (Isa. 66:24).

As the long ages of the past are succeeded by the ages to come, the church will meet its destiny as the greatest manifestation of God's grace. He has made us to sit together in heavenly places in Christ Jesus, "that in the ages to come he might shew the exceeding riches of his grace in his kindness toward us through Christ Jesus" (Eph. 2:7). As eternity replaces time, we shall reign with Christ over his universe forever and ever (Rev. 22:5).

APPENDIXES

APPENDIX 1
THE STUDY
OF BIBLE PROPHECY

The study of prophecy can be of great value to believers. It can release us from fear of the future (Matt. 24:6; Luke 21:26) and give us the wisdom necessary to understand what will happen in the "time of the end" (Dan. 12:9, 10).

Such study has sanctifying power: "Every man that hath this hope in him purifieth himself, even as he is pure" (1 John 3:3). Our faith is strengthened by it. Christ said to his disciples, "I have told you before it come to pass, that, when it is come to pass, ye might believe" (John 14:29). It stimulates prayer and communion with God. For example, when Abraham learned of the impending judgment on Sodom and Gomorrah, he gave utterance to the first intercessory prayer of the Bible (Gen. 18:20-33). Jeremiah's prophecy of the restoration of the Jews from their Babylonian captivity became the basis for Daniel's great prayer (Dan. 9).

The study of prophecy also motivates us to faithful Christian service. There is nothing unspiritual about looking forward to the rewards God has promised us. Even Moses "had respect unto the recompense of the reward" (Heb. 11:26). It is our privilege to strive for an incorruptible crown through the practice of godly self control (1 Cor. 9:25).

If it is to be profitable, our study of prophecy must be guided by the established basic principles of Bible study. An important truth is that the Bible was written for the people of God. It cannot be properly understood by anyone else. "The natural man receiveth not the things of the Spirit of God:

for they are foolishness unto him: neither can he know them, because they are spiritually discerned" (1 Cor. 2:14). The "natural man" is any individual, no matter how brilliant or well taught, whose mind has not yet been illuminated as the result of a personal transaction with Jesus Christ. "The preaching of the cross is to them that perish foolishness; but unto us which are saved it is the power of God" (1 Cor. 1:18).

God wants his people to understand what he has written for them. He has given us a revelation, not a concealment of truth. Some portions of Scripture are hard to understand (2 Pet. 3:16), but most of the Bible is written so plainly any Christian can grasp its meaning. The Bible says that we should read and meditate on the Word of God. God has given us his Spirit "that we might know the things that are freely given to us of God" (1 Cor. 2:12).

Interpret the text literally. The first principle governing successful Bible study is that we must take the text as it is, in its plain literal meaning. Some Christians "spiritualize" or allegorize what they read. They do not accept what it says. But it is wrong to rob Scripture of its simple and obvious sense. The normal, plain meaning of the language should be taken as the message God wants to convey, unless the context clearly shows it is an allegory or a figure of speech. In other words, when the plain sense makes good sense, we should seek no other sense.

Luther wrote, "The literal meaning of Scripture is the whole ground of faith." Melancthon advised his students, "Adhere to the simple grammatical sense . . . the plain, natural sense of Scripture always carries with it the richest and most valuable instructions." There has never been a fulfillment of Bible prophecy that was not literal. For example, more than twenty prophecies can be found which spoke of the day when the Lord was crucified: he was to be sold for thirty pieces of silver (Zech. 11:12); his hands and feet were to be pierced (Ps. 22:16); lots were to be cast for his garments (22:18); he was to be buried in a rich man's grave (Isa. 53:9). All these were fulfilled literally. There is absolutely no reason why prophecies related to his second coming should not be understood literally.

Respect the text. It is important to respect the Bible's every word. One of the most disturbing examples of disregard for the words of the Bible is seen in the popular notion that "Israel" and "the church" are synonymous terms. To assume that the Old Testament means the church when it speaks of Israel, or that the church is Israel under a different name in the New Testament, is to bring confusion to Bible study.

Watch the context. Another principle of Bible study, often neglected, is the necessity for observing the context in which a verse appears. Miles Coverdale, who prepared a translation of the Bible in 1535, said, "It shall greatly help ye to understand Scripture if thou mark not only what is spoken or written, but of whom, and to whom, with what words, at what time, where, to what intent, with what circumstances, considering what goeth before and what followeth."

It would be ridiculous to lift Job 2:4 out of its context, then quote it as the teaching of Scripture. The verse says, "All that a man hath will he give for his life." These are Satan's words, spoken in an effort to deceive. Nor would it be right to say the Bible teaches, "There is nothing better for man, than that he should eat and drink" (Eccles. 2:24). This was the uninspired opinion of Solomon about what he saw of life "under the sun," before recognizing the need for taking God— who lives above the sun—into account.

Beware of interpretation that leads to contradiciton. Second Peter 1:20 says, "No prophecy of the scripture is of any private interpretation." It has also been translated, "a matter of one's own interpretation." This is a warning against holding an opinion about a single verse or paragraph of prophecy which tends to contradict other passages dealing with the same theme. Our understanding of any part of the total revelation about any particular subject must be consistent with the whole. If our opinion about the meaning of one passage seems to do violence to the teaching of other Scriptures, then it is open to question, and further study is called for.

Study the order of events. Nothing is more certain than the order in which major events in the divine program are to take place. The Word tells us precisely how history will unfold. It presents many outlines of the way one event is to follow another in a definite chronological sequence.

When the first great outline of Israel's future history (Deut. 28–30) is compared to the first detailed New Testament outline (Matt. 24, 25), they are seen to be strikingly parallel. God told Moses what would befall the Jews, from their conquest of Canaan to the coming of the messianic kingdom. Much of this prophecy has long since been fulfilled, but four outstanding events still remain. They are to occur in the following order: (1) in their latter days the people of Israel, scattered all over the world, will remember and honor God's word to Moses (Deut. 30:1, 2); (2) the Lord will return; (3) he will "gather thee from all the nations, whither the Lord thy God hath scattered thee . . . and the Lord thy God will bring thee into the land which thy fathers possessed, and thou shalt possess it" (30:3-5); and (4) he will bless the Jews in their land during the kingdom age (30:5-10).

The first extended New Testament prophecy is known as the Olivet Discourse. It is primarily a revelation of what will happen to the Jews. The themes revealed to Moses reappear, with considerable new truth, but there is no departure from the orderly sequence introduced in Deuteronomy.

These two prophetic pictures, taken from widely separated parts of the Bible, are representative of many others (notably, Zech. 12–14; Rev. 19). Not every passage refers to the four themes introduced in Deuteronomy, but when two or more of these appear in any single passage, they are always in the same order. The other subjects frequently added to the total body of revealed truth are usually related to one of them. As all of Scripture is examined, a complete picture of the divine program emerges, clear and definite enough to provide the key to passages which might otherwise be obscure.

A second element in prophecy that helps clarify the order of coming events is the frequent occurence of time words—expressions that explain when something will occur and how it relates to other things in the divine plan. Time words include terms and phrases such as "in those days," "after many days," "then," "in the latter days," and "immediately after."

Start a small reference library. It is not necessary to have a large library for top-notch prophetic study. A handful of books, wisely used, can help any student not only to master the major themes, but to discover new truths that others have overlooked. One of the most useful volumes is *Strong's Exhaustive Concordance of the Bible* (Nelson, Abingdon, 1977), edited by James Strong and other scholars, first published in 1822 after one hundred men worked for thirty years to produce it. In the first section of 1340 pages, every word found in the King James Version is listed in regular order, and part of each verse is quoted where the word occurs. Beside each quotation is a number which refers to an excellent treatment of the original Hebrew and Greek found in dictionaries included at the back of the book.

Students who want further information about the meanings of the words in the original languages can find it in Genesius' Hebrew lexicon, or in the *Greek-English Lexicon of the New Testament* (by J. H. Thayer, Zondervan, 1956). More recent works are readily available.

Some students prefer the outstanding *Young's Analytical Concordance of the Bible* (by Robert Young, Eerdmans, 1955). This concordance differs from *Strong's* by listing each English word under its Hebrew or Greek original, which is briefly defined.

Nave's Topical Bible (Moody, 1975) is another extremely useful work for the serious student. Verses are listed by topics instead of words, and they are usually printed in their entirety. Every important passage on every important topic in the Bible is listed.

For background material about any subject treated in the Scriptures, a Bible dictionary or encyclopedia is needed. Consulting a different translation of the Bible sometimes throws new light on a particular passage. Commentaries are often useful, providing excellent help on the meanings of words in the original text. Many of them, however, deal with the obvious, or are based on theological systems which reject the literal meaning of most prophetic passages.

APPENDIX 2
PETER'S
PROPHETIC WARNINGS

Just before laying down his pen for the last time, the apostle Peter wrote four admonitions for Christians. He emphasized the importance of Bible prophecy in the life of every Christian. Peter says prophecy should play a vital role in Bible comprehension, soul-winning, sanctification, and growth in grace.

Peter's words serve as a fitting introduction—and conclusion—to the study of prophetic Scripture. If we heed his words, we will be mindful of what the prophets have written, we will do what we can to advance the cause of world evangelism, and we will live according to the divine Word.

> This is my second letter to you, dear brothers, and in both of them I have tried to remind you—if you will let me—about facts you already know: facts you learned from the holy prophets and from us apostles who brought you the words of our Lord and Savior.
>
> First, I want to remind you that in the last days there will come scoffers who will do every wrong they can think of, and laugh at the truth. This will be their line of argument: "So Jesus promised to come back, did he? Then where is he? He'll never come! Why, as far back as anyone can remember everything has remained exactly as it was since the first day of creation."
>
> They deliberately forget this fact: that God did destroy the world with a mighty flood, long after he had made the heavens by the word of his command, and had used

the waters to form the earth and surround it. And God has commanded that the earth and the heavens be stored away for a great bonfire at the judgment day, when all ungodly men will perish.

But don't forget this, dear friends, that a day or a thousand years from now is like tomorrow to the Lord. He isn't really being slow about his promised return, even though it sometimes seems that way. But he is waiting for the good reason that he is not willing that any should perish, and he is giving more time for sinners to repent. The day of the Lord is surely coming, as unexpectedly as a thief, and then the heavens will pass away with a terrible noise and the heavenly bodies will disappear in fire, and the earth and everything on it will be burned up.

And so since everything around us is going to melt away, what holy, godly lives we should be living! You should look forward to that day and hurry it along—the day when God will set the heavens on fire, and the heavenly bodies will melt and disappear in flames. But we are looking forward to God's promise of new heavens and a new earth afterwards, where there will be only goodness.

Dear friends, while you are waiting for these things to happen and for him to come, try hard to live without sinning; and be at peace with everyone so that he will be pleased with you when he returns. And remember why he is waiting. He is giving us time to get his message of salvation out to others. Our wise and beloved brother Paul has talked about these same things in many of his letters. Some of his comments are not easy to understand, and there are people who are deliberately stupid, and always demand some unusual interpretation—they have twisted his letters around to mean something quite different from what he meant, just as they do the other parts of the Scripture—and the result is disaster for them.

I am warning you ahead of time, dear brothers, so

that you can watch out and not be carried away by the mistakes of these wicked men, lest you yourselves become mixed up too.

But grow in spiritual strength and become better acquainted with our Lord and Savior Jesus Christ. To him be all glory and splendid honor, both now and forevermore. Good-bye.

(2 Peter 3, TLB)